I've known Fleur since our Ogilvy days, and I consistently saw her perform at an extraordinary level, delivering outstanding results even when the stakes were sky-high. Reconnecting recently, it was truly inspiring to witness how she's channelled that intensity, transforming it into a powerful engine for sustainable impact. Her new book, *The Overachiever's Reset,* is precisely what so many leaders need: a practical guide to building truly fulfilling careers without the constant threat of self-sacrifice. This isn't just a book; it's a critical conversation our industry has been waiting for.

—**Marie-Claire Barker,** Global Chief People Officer, WPP

I worked with Fleur on the Qantas rebrand whilst she was navigating treatment—and she showed up, gave it everything, and delivered like the professional she is. It blew me away. When she shared her story with my marketing team at the time, it changed how they thought about leadership and success. *The Overachiever's Reset* is what every leader needs to build sustainable teams and businesses that actually last.

—**Stephanie Tully,** Chief Executive Officer, Jetstar

I heard Fleur speak over a decade ago and her story stayed with me—then our paths crossed again recently and I watched how she'd transformed through such adversity to create real impact. *The Overachiever's Reset* is the book I wish every high performer drowning under unrelenting standards could read.

—**Suzana Ristevski,** CMO Google Australia & NZ

So much leadership development focuses on doing more, pushing harder, proving yourself to others. *The Overachiever's Reset* does the opposite and that's why it matters. It's a thoughtful, practical guide to let go of the need for external validation and, instead, lead effortlessly from a place of deep self-knowledge and authentic strength.

—**Sherilyn Shackell,** Founder & Global CEO, The Marketing Academy

I've had a front-row seat to Fleur's astonishing transformation—watching her lead with impact while navigating serious illness, always showing up and delivering excellence, then reshaping her entire career from agency leadership to helping other leaders avoid the same fate. What makes *The Overachiever's Reset* powerful is how it shows you can pursue ambitious goals with the good kind of power—the type that doesn't require you to betray yourself or sacrifice what matters most. Her profound story combined with this proven blueprint will help so many leaders find their way to sustainable success.

—Rose Herceg, WPP President, Australia and NZ,
Author, Leading Social Forecaster and Futurist

I've been that overachiever quietly breaking under impossible self-imposed standards—and I've watched brilliant founders do the same. Fleur's story is the wake-up call we need. This isn't another hustle-harder playbook. It's raw, real and gives you the sustainable blueprint to achieve your wildest ambitions without sacrificing yourself. Read this before you break.

—Lisa Messenger, Author, Founder and Lifestyle Entrepreneur

Stop performing your worthiness through endless achievement—you're already enough. Fleur gives you permission to reclaim yourself, take up space, and build success that doesn't cost you everything. This book is the wake-up call every overachiever needs before they break.

—Erika Cramer, The Queen of Confidence, Author,
Speaker, Creator of *The Confidence Chronicles*
Podcast, Coach and Psychotherapist

Fleur and I share a mission: helping leaders break free from the limiting beliefs that keep them exhausted and stuck. *The Overachiever's Reset* tackles what awareness alone can't solve – giving leaders the practical tools to interrupt unconscious patterns and lead from a place of integrity and authenticity. This is the bridge so many self-aware leaders have been waiting for.

—**Michael Bunting,** Speaker, Author, Researcher

This isn't just another personal development book—it's a wake-up call for high-achieving women who've spent too long chasing external validation, all while slowly losing themselves in the process. Fleur's journey is raw, real and utterly relatable, because she's lived the collapse and rebuilt from the inside out. *The Overachiever's Reset* is the blueprint we didn't know we needed—a call to stop performing, start listening, and finally lead from a place of enoughness. I've had the privilege of walking beside Fleur as she stepped into her truth, and this book is the permission slip for so many others to do the same.

—**Janine Garner,** Author, Speaker, Business Mentor

A beautifully honest and powerful book for anyone stuck in the relentless cycle of doing more and feeling less. Fleur Marks offers a compassionate wake-up call and a roadmap to success that no longer comes at the cost of your health, relationships or sense of self. Essential reading for modern high performers.

—**Sarah Grynberg,** Founder of Greatness Productions, Speaker, Author & Creator of *A Life Of Greatness* Podcast

I had the privilege of coaching Fleur through part of her transformation — witnessing the grit and grace it took to reimagine success and let go of performance-driven leadership. This book is the gift of that journey: vulnerable, practical and deeply needed. *The Overachiever's Reset* is a lifeline for any leader who's ever felt like they have had to earn their worth.

—**Jo Wagstaff,** International Coach, Bestselling Author of *Lead Like You,* Speaker

Sometimes it takes tragedy to wake us up. For me, losing my husband to cancer at 54. For Fleur, nearly losing everything proving she was enough. Now she's dedicated her work to helping overachievers stop making the same mistake — and this book is the blueprint. For every leader who's been so busy achieving they've forgotten to actually live, you must read this extraordinary book. Ask yourself whether your definition of success is costing you too much, and follow Fleur's advice to listen to the whispers before they become screams. Because life is too damn short, and later might be too late.

—**Kate Christie,** Bestselling author of *The Life List*

I've spent 25+ years working with brilliant marketing leaders across the region — creative, driven exceptional at transforming brands. But too many are quietly exhausting themselves in the process. *The Overachiever's Reset* addresses what our industry rarely discusses: how to sustain high performance without sacrificing yourself. Part powerful story that wakes you up to what really matters, part practical framework — this is essential reading for passionate marketers questioning the cost of their ambition.

—**Wendy Walker,** Chief Marketing Officer, President IAA Singapore, Top 100 CMO, Author

THE OVER-ACHIEVER'S RESET

THE OVER-ACHIEVER'S RESET

A BETTER WAY **TO SUCCEED** WITHOUT LOSING YOURSELF

FLEUR MARKS

WILEY

First published 2026 by John Wiley & Sons Australia, Ltd

© John Wiley & Sons Australia, Ltd 2026

All rights reserved, including rights for text and data mining and training of artificial intelligence technologies or similar technologies. Except as permitted under the *Australian Copyright Act 1968* (for example, a fair dealing for the purposes of study, research, criticism or review) no part of this publication may be reproduced, stored in a retrieval system, or transmitted, in any form or by any means, electronic, mechanical, photocopying, recording or otherwise. Advice on how to obtain permission to reuse material from this title is available at http://www.wiley.com/go/permissions.

The right of Fleur Marks to be identified as the author of *The Overachiever's Reset* has been asserted in accordance with law.

ISBN: 978-1-394-39491-3

A catalogue record for this book is available from the National Library of Australia

Registered Office
John Wiley & Sons Australia, Ltd. Level 4, 600 Bourke Street, Melbourne, VIC 3000, Australia

For details of our global editorial offices, customer services, and more information about Wiley products visit us at www.wiley.com.

Wiley also publishes its books in a variety of electronic formats and by print-on-demand. Some content that appears in standard print versions of this book may not be available in other formats.

Trademarks: Wiley and the Wiley logo are trademarks or registered trademarks of John Wiley & Sons, Inc. and/or its affiliates in the United States and other countries and may not be used without written permission. All other trademarks are the property of their respective owners. John Wiley & Sons, Inc. is not associated with any product or vendor mentioned in this book.

Limit of Liability/Disclaimer of Warranty
While the publisher and author have used their best efforts in preparing this work, they make no representations or warranties with respect to the accuracy or completeness of the contents of this work and specifically disclaim all warranties, including without limitation any implied warranties of merchantability or fitness for a particular purpose. No warranty may be created or extended by sales representatives, written sales materials or promotional statements for this work. This work is sold with the understanding that the publisher is not engaged in rendering professional services. The advice and strategies contained herein may not be suitable for your situation. You should consult with a specialist where appropriate. The fact that an organisation, website, or product is referred to in this work as a citation and/or potential source of further information does not mean that the publisher and author endorse the information or services the organisation, website, or product may provide or recommendations it may make. Further, readers should be aware that websites listed in this work may have changed or disappeared between when this work was written and when it is read. Neither the publisher nor author shall be liable for any loss of profit or any other commercial damages, including but not limited to special, incidental, consequential, or other damages.

Cover design by Wiley
Cover Images: © Popskraft//stock.adobe.com
© nevodka.com/stock.adobe.com

Set in 11/16pt and Utopia Std by Straive, Chennai, India.

SKY69B3E559-FCFF-4B1B-89DD-EBBC630585F3_040226

You are a disco ball — not because you're broken, but because you're multifaceted. The smooth surfaces and the rough edges, the polished victories and the messy struggles. Every experience that has shaped you creates a surface that catches light differently. It is in embracing all these facets of your journey that your magnificence truly shines, casting brilliance in every direction.

*To my greatest loves — Pete, Isabella and Luca. We are a fiercely close
family who held on tight to each other when life tested us.
Our bond is unbreakable.*

*Pete: My rock for over 30 years. You've shown me that love — real,
messy, imperfect love — is all we really need. I could not do life
without you walking this wild ride with me.*

*Isabella and Luca: You are my breath, my aroha and my reason for
everything. In the darkest moments, you were the light that kept me
going. You've taught me what unconditional love truly means and
shown me that being real is better than being perfect.
I am so proud of you my darlings.*

*To Kimlee, my sister: Taken too soon by Covid. You were my biggest
cheerleader — loving me and having my back no matter how different
our worlds were. I wish you were here to see this book.*

*And to you: If you're reading this because something whispered 'there
has to be a better way'. You're right. There is.*

CONTENTS

ABOUT FLEUR MARKS

Fleur Marks is a high-impact leadership trainer, author and keynote speaker who helps ambitious leaders achieve sustainable success without losing themselves in the process.

After building a successful global career leading agencies and some of the world's top brands, Fleur was diagnosed with a chronic incurable autoimmune disease. She has spent the last 15 years figuring out how to achieve extraordinary results without sacrificing everything that matters, while still being in a sick body.

Her approach blends neuroscience, behavioural psychology and real lived experience to deliver leadership programs that have helped thousands of leaders learn to achieve extraordinary results while showing up authentically, leading with impact, and retaining the energy to actually enjoy the success they create — without sacrificing their health, relationships or sense of self.

Fleur holds a Bachelor of Commerce and a Master of Commerce with First Class Honours. She's a sought-after keynote speaker and the founder of fleurmarks.com.au.

When she's not delivering programs that change lives, you'll find her practising conscious joy, wearing sequins, prioritising what lights her up, and acting as living proof that there is a better way — one that prioritises what brings you joy and transforms both how you lead and how you live.

Find her at:

fleurmarks.com.au

fleur@fleurmarks.com.au

Instagram: @fleurjmarks

LinkedIn: linkedin.com/fleurmarks

INTRODUCTION: I THOUGHT I WAS SUPERWOMAN … MY BODY HAD OTHER PLANS

By the time I was 35, I'd achieved everything I'd set out to prove.

First member of my family to get a degree. Youngest female executive leader. Bought my first house at 21. Regional agency client leader managing one of the world's most prestigious brands (American Express) across the Asia-Pacific region. I was travelling from Sydney to Singapore to London, navigating time zones, leading cross-cultural teams, making strategic decisions that impacted millions of customers.

I was the definition of an overachiever.

Early on, it felt brilliant. Whatever I aimed for, I went beyond — achieving what others couldn't, making the extraordinary look effortless, delivering excellence in every part of my life. In my mind, if I wasn't pushing the absolute limits, it wasn't really worth pursuing. I set the benchmark for myself very high.

My unrelenting standards got me what I wanted to reach my definition of success.

I thought I was Superwoman. Invincible. Valued for what I delivered.

On the outside, I had made it. Mastering the balancing act of being a mum, pursuing my career ambitions and having a life (occasionally).

But here's what no-one tells you about being an overachiever: The chase never ends. There's always one more goal, one more standard to meet, one more version of yourself you need to prove you can be.

The reset that wasn't

When the opportunity came to leave my big role in Singapore for a simpler role in Sydney, I thought I was making the change that would finally bring balance. One client, one market. Less chaos, more space.

I had a beautiful home, two amazing kids, a loving husband who held down the fort so I could run full tilt at my dreams. I genuinely loved my work, and thrived in the world of big ideas, creativity and high-stakes problem-solving, helping global brands win hearts (and wallets).

On the surface, I had it all.

Almost as soon as I landed back in Sydney, the client told us they were putting their business to pitch. The pace picked up, and I went straight back into overdrive and my old behaviours of delivering and performing.

Every day was full: full of meetings, deliverables, decisions. Pushing myself relentlessly to meet the high expectations I'd set for myself, never once questioning the cost. Because deep down, I believed the deal I'd made: I provide. I perform. I hold it all together. I deliver no matter what.

Sound familiar?

My kids were in private school. My husband was pivoting careers. We lived in a home that looked like success. So I wore the badge of 'busy' with pride, even as the cracks widened.

I was the main income earner; I had to keep going.

Yet, inside? I was completely and utterly wiped.

I underestimated the energy toll of changing countries, changing jobs, settling the kids into a new life. On the outside, I looked successful — the fabulous wardrobe, the fancy car, exotic trips away, the 'good' life. Yet, I had fallen back into my old trap of working myself to the bone.

The body keeps score

My diary was full, but inside, I was empty. The art of making everything look effortless was exhausting me. If I wasn't *doing*, I was lost. I was addicted to the chase, the rewards, the life I had carefully curated.

My body was screaming. The signs were everywhere — bones that ached in ways I couldn't explain, breathlessness that wouldn't quit, fatigue that felt like drowning — but I chose to ignore them all. I had too much to do. Too much to prove. Too many people depending on me.

I just kept going.

Because that's what we do, isn't it? We don't slow down. We don't question. We hustle, we push, we double down. We go beyond the ordinary to achieve the extraordinary. But in the process, we lose ourselves, and we don't stop to consider whether the success we're chasing is actually worth it.

Not until something stops us.

When everything breaks

For me, that 'something' was a rare, incurable autoimmune disease. Multi-organ stage 4 sarcoidosis in my lymph nodes, which are everywhere in your body. This disease was the kind that doesn't get better. The kind that has no cure.

Let me explain what this actually meant, because most people have never heard of sarcoidosis. Your immune system, designed to protect you, turns against you, creating inflammatory cells that form granulomas (clusters of immune cells) throughout your body. In my case, these granulomas were attacking multiple organs simultaneously.

The disease was so out of control, the medical team had to go hard or I wouldn't make my 40th birthday.

So began the assault on my body: urgent surgery, 23 rounds of chemotherapy (a cancer patient usually has six, so almost four times the norm). Each infusion left me violently ill, unable to function, with my body betraying me in ways I never imagined possible. There were countless immunotherapy infusions over the years that followed. Multiple surgeries. Thousands of pills. Years stuck in bed.

The steroids (designed to reduce the inflammation ravaging my organs) turned me into someone I didn't recognise. They triggered an out-of-body rage I couldn't control and a hunger that felt insane, making me crazy and driving me to eat everything in sight. The weight piled on: 30 kilograms that transformed my body completely. I didn't recognise myself in the mirror. My hair fell out. My face swelled beyond recognition. I looked like someone else entirely.

Here's what nobody prepares you for: I went from leading a team of brilliant minds across multiple markets, making strategic decisions that impacted millions, being the person everyone called when things needed to get done to a life that revolved around three things: the doctor, the dog and the postie.

That was it. That was my world.

My definition of success went from having it all to just wanting to survive the year. To stand long enough each day to kiss my kids goodnight. To be in a well body — something I'd taken completely for granted my entire life.

I lost my career identity overnight. I went from agency leader to 'N/A' on forms. From someone constantly in demand to someone who couldn't even get out of bed.

The complete collapse

It wasn't just my health that collapsed. Our entire life imploded.

The family business model we'd built our lives upon (me working full tilt while my husband held down the fort) collapsed along with my body. Without my income, our financial foundation crumbled. We lost everything I had defined as success: the house, the fancy car, the life that looked good from the outside. We couldn't even keep a roof over our heads.

I was forced to keep working through treatments just to try to survive financially, which meant I had to learn how to become a high-performing sick person. Fortunately, because it was an invisible illness, most people had no idea how sick I really was.

I had to figure out a way to show up and lead while navigating brutal treatments that left me barely functioning. To deliver results while my body was being poisoned to stay alive.

I was trying to navigate all of this while raising two small children who needed their mum. Our life was in crisis on every front: financial, physical, emotional.

For the first time in my life, I couldn't achieve my way out of this one.

No amount of effort, planning or relentless pushing would fix a body that had fundamentally broken. No strategic thinking would cure an incurable disease.

In the race to overachieve, we forget what truly matters — until it nearly costs us our life.

All that striving. All those achievements. All that worth I'd been trying to prove? None of it mattered if I couldn't be present for the life I'd been too busy building to actually live.

The words that shatter everything

Then came the news that broke me completely: It had spread to my brain.

'Prepare for the worst', they told me.

I was 40 years old facing the terrifying possibility that I might not see my children grow up, marry, have children of their own. It shattered everything I believed about strength, success and what truly matters.

The questions I'd been avoiding

You might be thinking this is another story about someone who worked herself sick. Yes, it is that, but it is so much more.

For over 15 years now, I've been sitting in the waiting room of death, where most people like me either get better or die. I've been given the greatest gift in the messy struggle of rebuilding my life despite it all.

Lying there, week after week, stuck in a sick body with my impermanence a reality, I was finally forced to ask the questions I had spent my whole life avoiding:

- If this is it… what do I actually want my life to be?
- Who am I without the striving or achieving?
- If I already felt enough, what would I choose then?

Heartbreakingly, I had no answers. I realised I had been living a life of expectation, not intention.

And then another blow

Then, just as I began to stabilise, came another blow: breast cancer. Another brutal chapter. Another Christmas in hospital. I wasn't meant to stay alive long enough to experience the side effects of my treatments, yet here I was, still living, with more strength than I ever knew I had.

And, somewhere in the wreckage, something beautiful cracked open.

The beginning, not the end

Having lost everything, I had to begin again. Not with another strategic plan or ambitious goal, but with radical honesty about what my version of success should really look like.

I stopped chasing a life that looked good on paper and started building a life that actually felt good to live.

No green juices were going to save me. This wasn't about optimising my morning routine or finding better productivity hacks. My first step of real transformation came around self-compassion and love. I had spent my entire life being my harshest critic, my most relentless taskmaster. I realised I had to do the deep inner work on my mindset because the beliefs that drove me, the patterns of behaviour that defined me and the costs I was willing to pay to achieve all needed to be reset.

I needed to shift my mindset around three fundamental things:

- being enough already
- stopping the endless performing
- letting go of the illusion of control.

Once I had begun that deep inner work, I needed to also set up my own operating system: a way to create impact while still being in a sick body on notice, not knowing when this could be 'it'. I needed to discover a way I could show up intentionally, live fully despite the limitations, and leave a lasting impact without sacrificing what remained of my health or losing myself again in the process.

Here's where the real story begins

I didn't just survive what should have killed me on multiple occasions. In the messy, hardest moments (facing countless treatments and daunting challenges), I figured out a better way.

For 15 years now, I've been dancing between chronic illness and leadership, hospital beds and boardrooms, proving that sustainable success is possible even when life is anything but certain. I've learned that there is a better way to achieve — and not at the cost of you.

I became a high-performing sick person, achieving within my limits in a way that allows me to live my best life, to take care of myself along the way and, more than that, to pursue a life of meaning and contentment.

This is a unique lens for overachievers like you who may be quietly wondering if the juggle and struggle are worth it.

I've spent over a decade redefining what ambition looks like when you finally understand your worth isn't something you earn — it's something you already have.

Why I'm telling you this

In my darkest moment of struggle, I made a decision: So while I'm still here, I'm determined to help others find the shortcut I never had: how to lead with impact, live fully, and stop losing themselves chasing 'enough'. When you stop leading for external approval and start leading from your own worth, everything changes. You create a bigger impact, not smaller. You lead better, not less. You finally feel free and deeply content without abandoning your ambition.

That is why I wrote this book.

This isn't just a personal story, it's a professional intervention. A wake-up call for leaders addicted to doing more without ever feeling more. It's the map I wish someone had handed me before my collapse, before my incurable diagnosis, before I forgot who I was and lost myself in the relentless *efforting*.

It's the legacy I'm leaving for every overachiever who's still sprinting on empty, hoping the next win will finally be enough. It won't be. But there is a better way.

You might be reading this because something inside you recognises the relentless pursuit you've been on. The constant proving. The feeling that no achievement ever feels like enough. The exhaustion of always having to be 'on'.

You're wondering if there's a way to be ambitious without sacrificing everything — most of all, you. To succeed without losing yourself. To finally feel like your accomplishments actually belong to you.

There is — and I'm living proof.

Your shortcut

This book isn't about slowing down or shrinking your ambition, it's about resetting: learning to achieve sustainably, lead authentically and finally feel worthy of the success you create without trying to overachieve.

I learned this the hardest way imaginable, and I do not want you to have to do the same. My very long road of redefining success can be your shortcut.

You don't have to break before you reset. Your ambition doesn't have to cost you everything.

There's a better way to succeed without losing yourself, and it starts with the first page you're about to turn.

Overachievers, are you ready to reset?

Love,

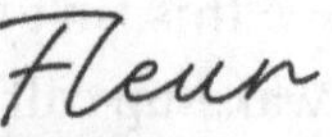

THE OVERACHIEVER'S CYCLE

You're exactly where you are meant to be.

You didn't end up here by accident. This book spoke to you in some way, telling you that something needs to change. Perhaps it's the exhaustion, the relentless proving, the juggle and struggle of navigating your ambition and trying to have a life as well. These aren't random struggles. They're the predictable outcome of a cycle most overachievers don't even know they're in.

Part I of this book is about raising your self-awareness, recognising where you are at right now and waking up to what you are experiencing so you can create real sustainable change. Helping you understand how you got here so you can make lasting meaningful change to achieve but not at the cost of yourself.

First, I want to reassure you: You're not broken. You're not failing at something others have mastered — you're an overachiever after all. You're simply operating within an impossible system that rewards over-functioning at the cost of yourself. That system starts with what you believe, drives how you behave and creates costs you're only beginning to recognise and want to change.

- ✧ *Chapter 1* shows you the unrealistic balancing act you're attempting, and why this tightrope was always designed to *break* you.
- ✧ *Chapter 2* reveals the five overachiever core *beliefs* that are driving you. The invisible beliefs about worth and success shape every high standard you set, every boundary you abandon, every version of yourself you sacrifice in pursuit of achievement.
- ✧ *Chapter 3* exposes the five behaviour *patterns* that you operate from. These behaviours are shaped by your belief system and have served you well, yet are not sustainable.
- ✧ *Chapter 4* delivers the *costs* and, ultimately, a wake-up call. What got you here will eventually break you. There are physical, emotional, relational and professional costs mounting while you're too busy achieving to notice.

This part will be uncomfortable. You'll recognise yourself in ways you've been avoiding, but recognition is where change begins. You can't solve a problem you can't see. You can't change patterns you don't recognise. You can't step off a tightrope you don't realise you're on. So let's start seeing clearly.

1

THE IMPOSSIBLE BALANCING ACT

Balancing on empty and calling it success

'Beware the busyness of a busy life.'

—*Socrates*

Everything to everyone

I was sitting in my driveway, car engine still running, unable to move.

The day was done. I'd delivered. Again. Nailed the presentation. Managed the crisis. Kept all the plates spinning. To everyone watching, I was the picture of competence, the woman who handles it all with grace and ease.

But sitting there, staring at my front door, I couldn't make myself go inside.

Because going inside meant being mum, wife, Fleur. The version of me who makes dinner and helps with homework and asks about everyone's day with genuine interest. And I had nothing left. Not one drop of genuine anything.

Then Carrie Underwood came on the radio with her song 'Take the Wheel', and something inside me cracked open.

Suddenly, tears were streaming down my face.

That song gave voice to something I'd been refusing to admit: I was in overload and overwhelm. I'd become so good at making the extraordinary look effortless that no-one (including me) had noticed I was going under.

I didn't want to face tomorrow's version of today. I didn't want this life I'd so carefully constructed any more. I wanted someone, anyone, to take control. To save me from the relentless performance I'd perfected. To take the wheel so I didn't have to keep showing up.

But sitting there in my driveway, I knew the truth: The only person who could save me was me.

This is what balancing precariously on empty looks like.

It's not dramatic, it's not obvious. It's just you, sitting in your car, too depleted to walk through your own front door. Too competent to admit you're drowning. Too proud to stop performing.

If you've ever felt this gap between how capable you appear to others and how close you are to complete and utter collapse, then you know exactly what I'm talking about. This is the tightrope — the tension between your ambition and it costing you everything.

You're not just busy. You're not just tired. Next week won't be any easier either. You're balancing on an unsustainable tightrope. One you and society have created. One you have been rewarded for, and one that is designed to break you.

The tightrope

You're 40 feet up. The rope frays under your feet, but you keep going because you're brilliant at this — making the extraordinary look effortless, solving what others can't, delivering beyond the norm, taking care of everyone's demands, achieving excellence no matter the challenge.

Your ambition keeps the rope taut, pulling you forward towards dreams that matter, impact you want to create, goals worth chasing. But the rope keeps extending. Rising higher. The wind picks up. You wobble but right yourself and keep going, because stopping feels like failure and slowing down feels like letting everyone down.

Every step feels precarious. You're caught between ambition demanding you keep going and your soul quietly begging you to stop. When you look ahead, there's no end in sight. Just more rope. Higher stakes. Bigger audiences expecting you not to fall.

You've built an impressive life. Perhaps it looks exactly like success should look. But somewhere, quietly, something doesn't quite feel right. You're beginning to question whether the rope you're on is the one you want to be on as it feels too high.

Maybe it's the relationships where you're physically present but mentally still at work. Or the moments when you catch a glimpse of who you used to be — someone who laughed more, dreamed without calculating the cost — and wonder where that version of you went.

Maybe it's the sense that you're exceptionally good at walking this tightrope, so good that stepping off feels like failure right now. Not because you can't, but because you've built so much and invested so much that stepping off would mean admitting it wasn't achievable all along.

Perhaps there's a small voice inside (the one you've been ignoring) that's whispering 'this isn't sustainable'. If that sounds familiar, then this chapter is for you.

The thing I learned too late is that the tightrope will eventually snap — not might — *will*.

My feet were blistered and bloody long before I fell. The signs were everywhere: exhaustion I pushed through, physical symptoms I ignored, relationships I sacrificed, the version of myself I kept abandoning. But I didn't step off. I thought I was invincible. I believed I was different. I convinced myself I could handle it and that it was worth it.

I kept walking until the rope broke beneath me.

You don't have to.

The sophistication of your balancing

Here's what made my situation so dangerous: I'd become exceptionally good at making the extraordinary look effortless.

From the outside, I had it all together. Regional role. Impressive title. The kind of career people aspire to. I managed teams across countries, handled crises with ease, delivered results that exceeded expectations. I was the person they called when they needed someone who could handle complexity without breaking a sweat.

This is the dangerous part about being an overachiever: We're so competent at managing the near-impossible that we convince ourselves (and everyone else) that it's actually possible.

I'd created a system that looked like excellence from the outside but felt like drowning from the inside. And because I made it look effortless, no-one questioned whether it was sustainable … including me.

The better I got at balancing the unrealistic expectations, the more challenges I took on. More responsibility. Bigger roles. Higher stakes. The system kept rewarding the performance, never asking what it cost to deliver it.

What a typical day looked like

Let me show you what 'having it all' and balancing my tightrope actually looked like.

The moment I woke up, I would jump out of bed and start running. Not literally but figuratively — from thing to thing, from role to role.

Jam start my day: Squeeze in exercise at 6 am, shower while mentally rehearsing the day's presentation, get ready to look the part (because appearing polished was non-negotiable), then get the kids ready, rush them to school while already on the phone, blow air kisses as they climbed out of the car.

By 9 am, I'd managed a crisis, packed two lunchboxes, responded to 14 emails and applied red lipstick in the car while navigating morning traffic. To anyone watching, I had it together.

Inside? I was already running on empty. I'd run a marathon before my actual work day even began.

Then came the meetings: back-to-back presentations to clients, solving crises, strategy sessions, leadership calls. Lunch eaten standing at my desk — or skipped entirely. More meetings. More firefighting. More decisions.

Race home for the kid routine: dinner, homework, bedtime stories delivered on autopilot while mentally drafting tomorrow's emails. The moment they were asleep, I'd jump back online for another hour or two, clearing the inbox, prepping for tomorrow.

Switch off the lights. Rinse and repeat.

Except I wasn't really switching off. I'd wake at 4 am, mind already churning through work problems.

It exhausts me even writing this. The pace. The energy. The momentum. No time to just be. Focused on outcomes always. What's next? Then next. Then next.

This was a pattern of behaviour I repeated five days a week, then I collapsed on weekends — too depleted to do anything meaningful, recovering just enough to start again Monday.

This was my normal. This is what high performers do, right?

This was what I called 'having it all'. This was the balancing act I'd perfected: being everywhere and nowhere, delivering excellence while losing myself, succeeding at everything except actually living.

And it was killing me. I just didn't know it yet.

You're not alone in this

The numbers tell the truth:

- 72 per cent of Australian women report complete exhaustion from the relentless juggle[1]
- 82 per cent of knowledge workers feel depleted[2]
- 68 per cent of parents in leadership positions report feeling guilt daily for neglecting family while striving for professional success.[3]

These aren't individual failures. This is systemic. A work culture and society that rewards achievement at the cost of you. You're not struggling because you're not good enough. You're struggling because the equation itself is unrealistic:

50+ hour work weeks + fully present parenting + personal health + showing up for relationships + maintaining your home + being the person everyone relies on+++

=

breakdown by default

Not *might* break down — *will*.

I know because I lived it. Let me show you what the balancing act actually looked like before it all came crashing down.

When resilience becomes self-abandonment

The better you get at making the superhuman look effortless, the more you think you can keep on pushing. I wore my resilience like a badge of honour. When others would have stopped, I kept going. Circumstances that would have broken most people, I found exhilarating and always found a way through believing it was my superpower.

I mistook my *capacity* to endure for evidence that I should. As a Māori woman, I'd been brought up on strength — a *wahine toa* (warrior woman) — someone who stands firm no matter what.

I thought of Mahuika, the goddess of fire. When Māui (the trickster demigod) demanded her flames, she gave him her fingernails of fire one by one, diminishing herself until she had almost nothing left. She kept everyone else warm while her own fire dimmed. That was me. Made of solid stuff, giving all of myself to everyone and everything, but burning out in the process.

When you can sustain the unsustainable longer than most, you stay on the tightrope longer. Push harder. Sacrifice more. The rope keeps extending. The stakes keep rising. The number of audiences expecting you not to fall keep growing.

The brutal irony? My resilience became the very thing keeping me on the tightrope long after I should have stepped off.

I remember getting seriously ill while on a work trip to San Francisco — my hair was falling out from stress, I couldn't get out of bed, my body was completely depleted. Did I cancel the meetings and stay in bed? No, I medicated myself through it, showed up to meetings looking professional and delivered what was needed. Because that's what resilient people do, right?

Wrong.

That's not resilience. That's overriding every signal your body sends because you've confused endurance with strength.

Real resilience is knowing when to bend. Knowing when to stop. Knowing the difference between pushing through a challenge and pushing yourself off a cliff. I didn't know the difference, I just kept pushing.

When I was going through chemotherapy treatment, which left me depleted for days, I'd be back at work within 48 hours, performing like nothing had happened. Colleagues would marvel at my dedication. 'You're so strong', they'd say, 'so inspiring'.

But I wasn't strong. I was terrified. Terrified that if I stopped, I'd get behind or be judged for being sick. Terrified I'd lose my value, lose my identity as the woman who could handle anything.

I remember returning from treatment cycles and immediately going into over-function mode, feeling guilty for stepping away when things were busy. I'd perform like I was making up for lost time, trying to convince my body (and everyone else) that I was 'fine'. Full intensity from day one, not recognising the cumulative cost of months of treatment and years of override.

This is what happens when you've trained yourself to ignore every signal that says 'stop' because stopping feels like failure. When you've built an entire identity on being the person who can handle anything, admitting you can't becomes existentially threatening.

So you keep going. Keep pushing. Keep proving. Until something breaks.

We've become so good at pushing through that everyone assumes we're 'fine'. We deliver flawlessly while falling apart. We make exhaustion look like excellence. And the system rewards us for it—with more responsibility, bigger roles, higher stakes. We never ask ourselves what it's actually costing us to maintain the performance.

When 'fine' becomes a red flag

Sitting there in my driveway, engine still running, I knew the truth: I was not fine.

I came to learn that 'fine' is the four-letter lie we tell ourselves. It's the ultimate overachiever deflection. The word we use when we're too exhausted to explain, too proud to admit we're struggling or too afraid that if we start being honest, everything will unravel.

Fine is efficient. Fine keeps people from asking follow-up questions. Fine protects everyone else from our reality and protects us from having to face it ourselves. It became my most used word. My default response. My protective shield for admitting how I really was to myself and others.

In fact, someone later told me what 'fine' really stands for:

F = Fucked up

Nothing was working. Not my energy. Not my relationships. Not the carefully constructed system I'd built. I was running on fumes and calling it resilience.

I = Insecure

What if I can't keep this up? What if I'm not actually as capable as everyone thinks? The tightrope felt safer than admitting I didn't have all the answers.

N = Neurotic

Obsessing over every detail, replaying every conversation, triple-checking everything. My brain wouldn't switch off. Relaxing felt dangerous.

(continued)

E = Emotionally unstable

One minute I was fine (or so I told myself), the next, I was crying in my car to a country song. My emotional bandwidth was shot. I had nothing left for contentment, connection or even basic patience.

When you're an overachiever, 'fine' becomes your default script. It's the response you say so convincingly that even you start to believe it.

But 'fine' isn't neutral. 'Fine' is a warning sign. I had to honestly face sitting in that driveway while realising that the only person who could get me off this tightrope was me.

No-one was coming to save me. No magical intervention was going to slow down my life. No-one else could see how desperately I needed help because I'd become brilliant at hiding it.

The tightrope was mine. And so was the choice to step off it.

The life you're missing while you're living it

High achievers don't mean to miss our lives while balancing 40 feet in the air, but we do.

You eat lunch at your desk, eyes on your screen, only looking down for your next bite, and realise you've already finished eating without tasting a thing.

You drive home after a long day and don't remember the journey at all. Thirty minutes vanished. Your body drove. Your mind was somewhere else entirely.

I've had moments where I was with my kids … but not really with them. My body was present, but my mind was deep in tomorrow's to-do list. They'd tell me something important, and I'd nod along, thinking I was listening until they'd ask me a question and I'd have to admit I hadn't heard a word.

I even remember working in Tokyo — flying in several days a week for five months to solve a major client issue. Five months in one of the most extraordinary cities in the world. And here's the thing: I couldn't tell you anything about my time there beyond the office and hotel room. The culture, the food, the streets, the people — it's all a blank. Just airport, office, hotel, repeat. I was physically in Tokyo, but I wasn't really there at all. Now, looking back, the loss feels staggering. Five months I'll never get back. An entire city I never experienced, all because I was too busy solving everyone else's problems to notice where I actually was.

Maybe your version looks different. Airport queues spent on calls. Dinner conversations interrupted by 'urgent' emails that could have waited. Family holidays where you're physically there but mentally still at the office.

The details change, but the pattern is the same. We don't even realise how disconnected we've become … until we do.

Whether it's a relationship breaking point, a health crisis you can't ignore or simply a moment (like me in that driveway) when you suddenly see the gap between the life you're living and the life you thought you were building.

This is the sneaky cost of tightrope living: The people you love get the version of you that's left over. The depleted you. The distracted you. The exhausted you who's given everything to everyone else and has nothing genuine left for them.

The real cost?

You miss the moments that actually matter while chasing the achievements that don't. People feel like they're never important enough because you're always distracted by the next thing. Relationships become built on performance and delivery rather than genuine connection. And, gradually, you erode your sense of what you actually want, so you just keep going, hoping things will change, because you've forgotten how to choose differently.

Your workplace rewards this behaviour. Outcomes and busyness become badges of honour. Your patterns are reinforced and validated, so you begin to believe this pace is simply what's expected. After all, isn't this what all high performers do?

And you begin to believe this is the only way, never questioning your reality as you go faster to deliver exceptional results. Until your sense of contentment erodes. Or your body shouts. Or you simply can't do it any more. And you realise that your self-worth is tied up in external validation through achieving, and the gap between public success and private emptiness has grown too wide to ignore.

Why this keeps happening

Here's what I didn't understand when I was on that tightrope: I wasn't just overloaded, I wasn't just overwhelmed, I was trapped in a cycle I couldn't see.

The tightrope wasn't sustainable. I didn't end up there by accident because I had been rewarded for my achievements that went beyond the call. I had fallen into a cycle that turns your greatest superpowers into your deepest life lessons. And once you see how it works, you can finally stop balancing on this precarious tightrope and start finding a better way to achieve not at the cost of you.

I call it The Overachiever's Cycle (Figure 1.1), and it has three stages that feed each other in an endless loop, tightening with every rotation.

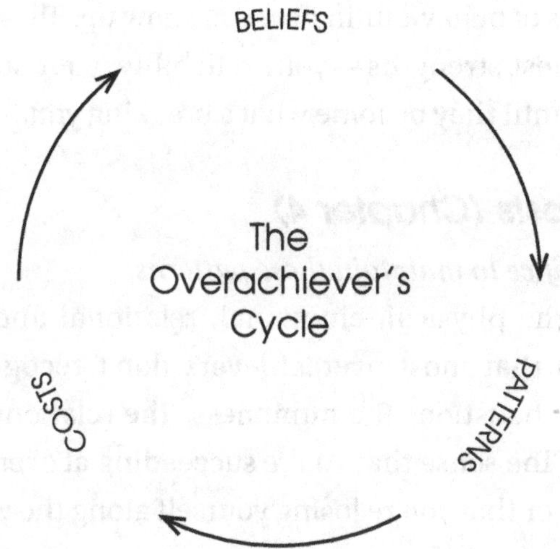

Figure 1.1 The Overachiever's Cycle

Stage 1: Beliefs (Chapter 2)

What you believe about yourself and success.

These are the invisible beliefs you absorbed from your family, upbringing, culture and conditioning. The ones that tell you that:

- your worth depends on what you achieve
- rest is something you earn
- asking for help is weakness
- you should be able to handle it all
- anything less than excellent is not good enough.

These beliefs drive every decision you make, every standard you set, every boundary you abandon.

Stage 2: Patterns (Chapter 3)

How you behave based on those beliefs.

The repeated behaviours (perfectionism, people-pleasing, over-functioning, pushing through) from Stage 1 become automatic repeat patterns of behaviour in how you show up. These patterns feel like your greatest strengths — your reliability, your standards, your dedication — until they become what's breaking you.

Stage 3: Costs (Chapter 4)

What you sacrifice to maintain those patterns.

These are the physical, emotional, relational and professional consequences that most overachievers don't recognise until it's too late. The exhaustion. The numbness. The relationships that feel transactional. The sense that you're succeeding at everything except actually living or that you're losing yourself along the way.

Here's why this matters:

- You can't solve a problem you can't see.
- You can't change patterns you don't recognise.
- You can't step off a tightrope you don't realise you're on.

The next three chapters will show you exactly how you got here, because once you see the cycle clearly, you can finally break it.

The tightrope isn't keeping you safe. It's keeping you trapped in a cycle where beliefs drive patterns that create costs that confirm your original beliefs. Fortunately, cycles can be broken, and that's exactly what we're about to do.

Let's start with what's driving everything: The beliefs you've been carrying that were never actually yours to begin with.

What I know to be true

✧ The hardest person to save is yourself because you're the one balancing on the rope, but you can step off at any time you choose.

- ✧ I thought if I could just balance better, work smarter, optimise harder, I'd make it work, but there is no 'making it work'. The tightrope isn't a challenge to master, it's a trap to escape.
- ✧ You're reading this book. That means some part of you already knows something needs to change. Trust that part. Tune into it.
- ✧ The tightrope you're on right now? It's not keeping you safe, it's keeping you precariously balanced at a cost to you. And the only person who can choose to step off is you. But first, you need to understand how you got up there in the first place.
- ✧ That's what the next three chapters are for. To help you understand how you ended up here and what needs to shift. Because once you see the cycle that put you on the tightrope, you can finally break it, and build something sustainable in its place.
- ✧ The question isn't whether you can keep balancing. The question is: Are you brave enough to step off?

Power pause: Your tightrope balancing act

Let's take a look at your daily tightrope walk. Let's reflect on those micro-moments where you choose to balance on your tightrope and convince yourself that you have to keep doing so. For every statement that you identify, give yourself 1 point.

This morning, you:

- ☐ checked your phone before your feet hit the floor
- ☐ jammed your morning full of tasks before you even got to the office

(continued)

☐ rushed feeling like you were already chasing the day even though it was only 8 am

☐ said 'just quickly' or 'hurry up' to someone you love

☐ multitasked through breakfast (or skipped it entirely)

☐ looked at your packed day and felt energised by being needed.

During your day, you:

☐ ate lunch in a meeting, dashing to your next thing or not at all

☐ answered emails during meetings as you can't afford to get behind

☐ stayed late 'just to get ahead for tomorrow'

☐ said 'I'm fine' or 'I'm busy' when someone asked how you are

☐ felt guilty for taking a toilet break or having a casual conversation with someone about nothing important.

With people you love, you:

☐ nodded along while mentally planning your to-do list

☐ felt impatient when others moved slowly or took longer than expected

☐ checked your phone during family time or straight after

☐ rushed through bedtime routines to get back to work

☐ struggled to be fully present with them because your mind was elsewhere.

When you reflect on your inner state, you:

☐ can't remember the last time you felt truly relaxed or did nothing

☐ feel accomplished when your diary is full of people needing you

☐ wear 'busy' like a badge of honour

☐ believe rest is something you earn…later

☐ feel guilty when you're not achieving something or delivering

☐ run on adrenaline more than actual energy

☐ tell yourself 'I'll slow down when…' (but that moment never comes).

What your score reveals

15+ points: You're not just on the tightrope, you're sprinting across it with blisters. Your nervous system is in constant overdrive, and you've normalised operating at a pace that isn't sustainable. You're exactly who this book is for.

10–14 points: You're living in the fast lane more often than not. You have fleeting moments of presence, but the pull back to performance is strong. The tightrope is getting harder to balance on and, deep down, you know it.

5–9 points: You catch yourself on the tightrope and occasionally step off, but consistency is the challenge. The patterns are there, even if they're not running the show yet. This is your warning signal.

0–4 points: Either you've already done the work to step off the tightrope and reclaim your pace, or you're not being fully honest with yourself yet. Overachievers are excellent at minimising what's really happening.

Here's the truth: If you gave yourself a point for more than half of those statements, you're not being resilient, you're walking a tightrope that's slowly fraying beneath you and calling it success and it's costing you you.

This isn't about judgement. It's about recognition. You can't step off the tightrope if you don't first admit you're on one.

✧ Glittering truths ✧

If you only remember three things from this chapter, make them these:

1. You're not failing at balance, you're succeeding at a near-impossible task

The tightrope you've been walking was never meant to be sustainable. The exhaustion you feel isn't proof you're not strong enough. It's proof the system itself is broken. Those moments when you feel like you're barely holding it together while everyone else seems fine? That's the illusion cracking open. Nobody is balancing it all. Some people are just better at hiding the wobble.

2. The sophistication of your suffering is what makes it so dangerous

You've become so good at making the extraordinary look effortless that everyone—including you—assumes you're fine. You deliver flawlessly while falling apart. You make exhaustion look like excellence. And the system rewards you for it with more responsibility, bigger roles and higher stakes. The better you get at the balancing act, the longer you can sustain the unsustainable, which means you stay on the tightrope longer, push harder, sacrifice more.

3. The tightrope isn't random, it's a cycle you can see and break

You didn't end up here by accident. There's a predictable pattern to how capable people end up exhausted. Beliefs drive patterns that create costs that confirm the original beliefs. Round and round, tightening with every rotation. But once you see the cycle clearly, you can finally interrupt it.

<u>2</u>

CYCLE STAGE 1: THE FIVE BELIEFS RUNNING YOUR LIFE

Understanding the core beliefs driving your overachievement

'Ko te piko o te māhuri, tērā te tupu o te rākau'.
[The way the sapling is shaped determines how the tree grows.] —*An ancient Māori* whakatauki (*proverb*)

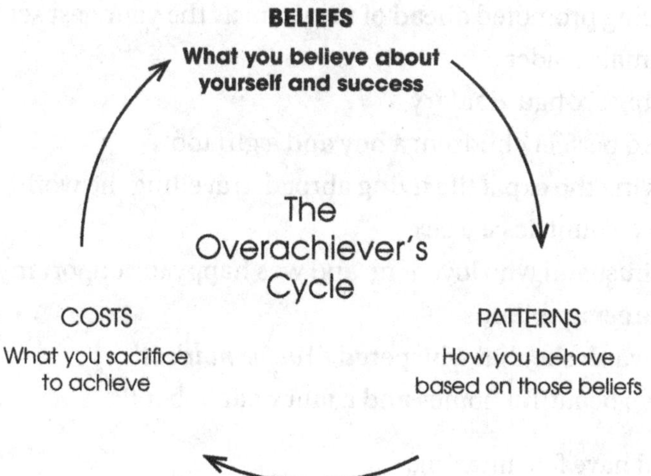

The belief that shaped everything

At 23, I was sitting at a leadership luncheon, and I asked a famous keynote speaker: 'How do you balance it all: the career, the life, the love, everything?'

She smiled, a little sadly. 'Darling, you don't.'

I refused to believe her. So I set myself a challenge: I would prove her wrong. After all, my mum had told me it was possible.

My mum raised me to believe that girls could do anything—and that we should. That her generation had fought for the choices mine could now enjoy. I didn't just want to live up to that promise, I wanted to exceed it.

Somewhere along the way, gold stars became my oxygen. I can still picture Mrs Crabtree, my primary school teacher, handing me a shiny sticker when my homework was the best in the class. I bloody loved those gold stars! Without realising it, I learned that approval, praise and achievement were the currency of my worth.

And for a while, it looked like I was worthy. By 35, I had checked every box success had promised. I was my definition of success with:

- an amazing career where I was respected
- being promoted ahead of my years as the youngest senior female leader
- a big six-figure salary
- two perfect children: a boy and a girl too!
- living the expat life living abroad: travelling the world, often two countries a week
- a husband who loved me and was happy to support my career ambitions
- a wardrobe that whispered, '*You've made it*'
- two beautiful homes and a fancy car to boot!

It should have felt amazing.

I just kept believing that in one more deadline, one more milestone, I would crack the code. I would figure out how to have it all soon … and then enjoy it.

Because high achievers don't stop, right? We sprint harder, double down, push further. I had built my life on beliefs that looked strong but were silently breaking me.

The high standards that made you excellent? They've become the measuring stick you'll never measure up to. The resilience that got you through hard times? It's turned into a refusal to admit when you're not fine.

I know this because I lived it. I built an entire career on beliefs I never questioned. And I didn't realise they were breaking me until I was too sick to keep going.

Your beliefs are the fuel keeping you on the tightrope. You didn't choose these beliefs, but you're living them. And the good news? You can rewire your brain to form new neural pathways at any age. Phew! But, first, you must understand what beliefs sit deep within you, driving your achievement while no longer serving you. You can't change what you can't see.

Like me, as an overachiever you've been operating on autopilot, driven by beliefs you've never questioned, beliefs that feel like facts but are actually just old stories on repeat.

We're moving so fast that we don't slow down long enough to notice the impact. Or we see the signs (the exhaustion, the emptiness) and choose to ignore them because stopping feels like exposure. The moment we pause, everyone will see we're not as capable as they thought. That we're fraudulent. That we've been one step away from being found out this entire time.

Researchers Pauline Clance and Suzanne Imes called this imposter syndrome[4]: that persistent self-doubt high achievers carry despite evidence of competence. For us, staying busy becomes a defence mechanism. If we're constantly proving ourselves, we won't have to face the fear underneath that we're not actually good enough.

Brené Brown's research[5] on perfectionism reveals what's really driving this. It's not about high standards, it's about fear. The deep-down terror that 'I am not enough'. So we make our worth conditional: I'm only valuable when I'm achieving. And rest? Rest threatens the entire equation because it removes the proof.

When you start catching these beliefs mid-thought — noticing when you tell yourself *I'm only valuable when I'm busy* or *rest is something I'll do later* — something shifts. You create space between the belief and your behaviour, and in that space, you get to choose differently.

This isn't just mindset work, it's neuroscience. Your brain has spent years wiring these beliefs into automatic responses through repetition. Every time you push through exhaustion, every time you say 'yes' when you mean 'no', you're strengthening that neural pathway. But here's the beautiful truth: you can rewire your thoughts. Neural pathways can change. Not overnight. Not perfectly. But consciously, deliberately, one choice at a time.

Once you see the invisible code running your life, you can finally start rewriting it. That's where real change begins, not in doing more, but in believing differently about what you're worth without the doing.

Your beliefs are running the show

No-one wakes up deciding to outrun their own life. It starts slowly, with invisible rules you absorb without realising. Work harder. Be better. Achieve more. Keep pushing. Only then will you be enough.

These rules become beliefs: stories about who we are, what we must do and what we need to be safe, successful or loved. We don't even realise we're living by them. They become the quiet code running in the background, shaping how we lead, love, achieve and rest.

Core beliefs sit deep within us, formed from our earliest experiences: what we saw, what we were rewarded for, what we feared. Over time, they harden into our inner operating system, influencing how we interpret feedback, handle uncertainty and measure our worth.

For overachievers, these beliefs are particularly treacherous. They masquerade as ambition or drive while slowly eroding our joy, health and sense of self. They promise fulfilment but deliver exhaustion.

Understanding what shaped us is where the reset begins. Once you see your belief system, you can rewrite it. Awareness is the first act of lasting change.

We create beliefs early and we learn them from parents, culture and environment. For example, I learned early that if I pleased my parents through achievements and did well at school, I was praised and loved. The good girl.

These beliefs form neural pathways that become our default setting. They become your brain's shortcuts. Once formed, our thoughts automatically follow them, making them feel like truths, even when they no longer serve you. Beliefs tied to achievement, self-worth and survival are especially hardwired; for example:

- If I don't do it, it won't get done properly.
- Rest is something I'll earn later when I've done enough.
- My worth lives in my productivity and being needed.
- Asking for help means I'm not capable.
- I have to prove myself. Every. Single. Day.

This belief system got you the promotions, the recognition, the life that looks successful. But somewhere along the way, these same beliefs stopped serving you and started consuming you.

The drive that made me unstoppable is also why I couldn't stop — even when my body was begging me to. If I stopped, I feared I'd no longer be worthy or lovable.

The 5 Ps of overachieving

After two decades of working with high performers (and living this hardwired internal operating system myself), I've identified five core beliefs that keep overachievers trapped on the tightrope. These aren't random thoughts. They form the operating system most ambitious, driven people are running on, often without realising it.

I call them the 5 Ps of overachieving.

These beliefs exist because your ambition is real. You genuinely want to create impact, serve others, build something meaningful. But the very drive that was supposed to fuel your success started consuming you instead. The beliefs that got you here became the ones keeping you stuck.

Until you see these beliefs clearly, you can't rewrite them. You need to be able to name it to tame it. In Part II, we will begin to shift these beliefs further, but for now, let's name the 5 Ps of overachieving.

1. Perfectionism: It has to be flawless or I'll fail

This is the belief that pushes us to constantly be better. You hit send on emails with 'sorry this isn't better' even when it's already brilliant. You'd rather miss a deadline than submit 97 per cent work because, in your mind, if it's not perfect, it's not ready. You stay up late polishing your team's presentation, not because it isn't already strong, but because you 'need' to add that extra shine. Your drafts folder is overflowing not with bad ideas, but with brilliant ones you've convinced yourself aren't ready to see the light of day. You rehearse presentations so many times you could recite them backwards, yet you still feel underprepared. You rewrite emails multiple times, agonising over whether 'Thanks' or 'Many thanks' was more professional.

The brain hook: Every perfect delivery triggers dopamine. Your brain rewards perfectionism, creating an addiction to flawless that's challenging to sustain.

2. People-pleasing: Everyone else first

This is the martyrdom trap disguised as loyalty. Everyone else's needs matter more than your own. 'Yes' tumbles out before your brain processes the request. You check your phone during your own birthday dinner 'just in case someone needs you'. You detect mood shifts from three time zones away and think it's something you've done.

You give advice you'd never follow yourself. You go on a well-earned holiday with your family but feel guilty, so you constantly check in despite telling your team you're unavailable. You play so many roles in your life you've lost track of who you actually are.

The cost: When everyone else gets your best, you get what's left ... which is usually nothing.

3. Proving: I must earn my worth through achievement

People need you. A full diary means I am in demand. Valued. Give a busy person something that needs to get done and they will do it. No task is too big or deadline too tight. Your worth feels tied to being needed, delivering, never standing still.

Your CV reads like you're applying to run the United Nations. Compliments make you more uncomfortable than root canal surgery. You're perpetually auditioning for your own life, seeking praise to sense-check whether it was exceptional or a failure. You believe that, in order to achieve, you must sacrifice yourself to get there.

The trap: External validation becomes your drug of choice, but the dose keeps needing to increase.

4. Performing: I must have it all together all the time

You must appear flawless. You've perfected looking boardroom-ready always. Your social media looks like you're living your best life, even when you're exhausted and haven't left the house all weekend. You're the go-to person for crises because you can handle everything.

'Fine' is your default response even when your world is on fire. You pretend to know the answer because admitting ignorance feels unacceptable.

The exhaustion: Performing takes massive energy, energy you need for actual leading and living.

5. Pushing through: Keep going, everything will get better soon

Hard work conquers all. You tell yourself 'It's just a busy period', or 'Things will calm down soon', or 'I just need to push through'. You keep postponing holidays, gym, sleep, healthy eating—your entire wellbeing—indefinitely.

Nothing good comes easy, right? You wear your ability to power through exhaustion like a badge of honour. Your lunch break is mythical.

You always show up to the meeting, the crisis, the deadline, even when your body is unwell because you don't have time to take a sick day. Rest feels like weakness. Slowing down feels like failure.

The breaking point: Your body keeps score and, eventually, it presents the bill.

What I know to be true

✧ You've been living by rules you never consciously chose. Working harder to feel worthy. Pleasing others to feel safe. Performing perfection to feel accepted. These aren't character flaws, they're survival strategies that worked until they didn't.

✧ The exhaustion you feel isn't because you're not strong enough, it's because you've been running software that demands unrealistic things: that your value be earned, that your place requires constant proof.

✧ There's nothing wrong with ambition. There's everything wrong with ambition that erases you. The beliefs driving you were never about excellence, they were about survival. You don't need to survive your life any more…you get to actually live it.

✧ Once you see these beliefs clearly, once you understand they're old programming, not facts, everything shifts. Not overnight. Not perfectly. But consciously. You start catching yourself mid-belief. Questioning the stories. Choosing different responses.

✧ This is where the real work begins: not in doing more, but in believing differently about what makes you enough. Now you've named the beliefs, let's see how they show up in your daily behaviour.

Power pause: Your 5 Ps

Grab your journal. Take a deep breath and reflect on which of the 5Ps has been running your life.

▸ Which of the 5 Ps is your dominant one: perfectionism, pleasing, proving, performing or pushing through?

▸ Where did it come from? Whose voice does it echo?

▸ How does it show up in your life as you achieve?

(continued)

- Is it serving you or costing you right now?
- Where does this belief tend to happen for you? At work? At home? Everywhere?

Be curious and kind to yourself as you explore what has shaped you.

Power pause: The belief catcher

Now you are aware of your dominant beliefs, the trick is catching them in action and naming them when they appear. Awareness is the first step to taming them. Changing them comes later in Part II.

Think about your last week. Really think about it. Be honest when you answer these questions:

- What did you redo that was already good enough? (*Perfectionism*)
- What did you say 'yes' to that you wanted to say 'no' to? (*People-pleasing*)
- What did you achieve that still didn't feel like enough? (*Proving*)
- What did you perform that you weren't actually feeling (on autopilot)? (*Performing*)
- What did you push through that your body asked you to pause for? (*Pushing through*)

If you feel ready, catch and name your beliefs as they appear throughout the week ahead, especially moments where you feel triggered or under pressure. Just notice gently and name it; for example, 'Oh, isn't that interesting. I am the only one here late because I offered to perfect that presentation.'

✨ Glittering truths ✨

If you only remember three things from this chapter, make them these:

1. Your beliefs aren't your fault but they are your responsibility

You didn't choose these stories about worth, success and safety, you inherited them from family, absorbed them from culture, earned them through experience. While you didn't write this code, you're the only one who can update it. No-one else can do this work for you.

2. These beliefs feel like truth, but they're just old stories on repeat

That voice saying 'you're not doing enough' isn't wisdom, it's childhood programming. The drive that says 'rest is weakness' isn't ambition, it's fear dressed up as excellence. Your brain has been running this code so long it feels like fact. But beliefs can be updated once you recognise them as stories, not truths.

3. Recognition without judgement is where transformation begins

These beliefs protected you once. They got you here. But what got you here won't get you there — wherever 'there' is for you. Catching these beliefs mid-thought, naming them when they arise, creates space between the belief and your behaviour. In that space, you get to choose a new way.

3

CYCLE STAGE 2: WHEN BELIEFS BECOME PATTERNS

How the beliefs transform into daily behaviours

> 'All that glitters is not gold.'
>
> — *William Shakespeare*

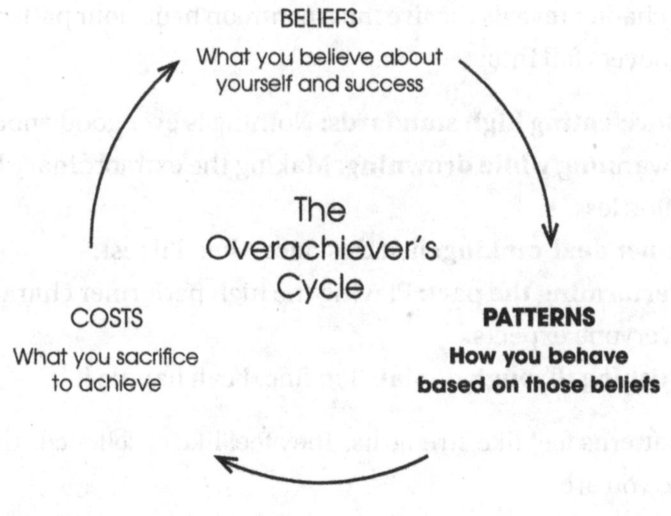

In Chapter 2, we named the five beliefs driving you (the 5Ps of overachievement). Now, let's see how they show up in your daily life. These beliefs don't just sit in your mind, they become patterns of behaviour on autopilot. Specific, predictable ways you act out what you believe about your worth.

Like Tāwhirimātea, the Māori god of winds and storms, whose winds blow in predictable patterns across the land, you can learn to recognise the patterns moving through your life. Once you see them clearly, you can choose whether to keep dancing to their rhythm or step into stillness.

What started as beliefs about success have become a part of the cycle you've built with your own hands, one productive day at a time. These patterns feel like strength but they're slowly diminishing the real you.

Here's how beliefs become patterns: In Chapter 2, you identified your dominant beliefs from the 5Ps (perfectionism, people-pleasing, proving, performing and pushing through). Those beliefs don't just sit in your mind, they become automatic behaviours — patterns you repeat without thinking, like walking the same path each day until you've worn a groove in the ground.

This chapter reveals the five most common behaviour patterns that overachievers fall into:

1. **Unrelenting high standards:** Nothing is ever good enough.
2. **Swanning while drowning:** Making the extraordinary look effortless.
3. **Inner deal-making:** Just this once, then I'll rest.
4. **Performing the part:** Playing the high performer character everyone expects.
5. **Pushing through denial:** 'I'm fine, I can handle it.'

These patterns feel like strengths. They feel like excellence. They feel like who you are.

But they're not. They're just old survival strategies on autopilot. Let me show you exactly how this plays out.

Behaviour pattern 1: Unrelenting high standards

In Chapter 2, I talked about how much getting a gold star for my work in primary school meant to me, and even then, I held myself to impossibly high standards. I always wanted to be the best: to achieve, to impress, to prove I was worth noticing.

As a child, my Dad was mostly absent, and, like many kids in broken families, I learned early that being 'good' earned praise. At school, if I achieved well and did my homework to perfection, I would be granted that coveted gold star. At university, I didn't settle for a bachelor's, I wanted a master of commerce with first-class honours and would not settle for less. In my first few roles, I was the youngest woman to achieve them. I wanted to be exceptional at everything I put my hand to, and anything less was simply not good enough.

From a very young age, I held impossibly high standards for myself. And these standards earned me gold stars, promotions, and praise from everyone who mattered.

My standards, along with my beliefs, pushed me to achieve amazing things. I was the good girl who always showed up, did my best and over delivered on *everything*. The world rewards this behaviour. It cheers your hustle, your sacrifice, your performance.

But here's what I didn't understand: This relentless drive to achieve the extraordinary wasn't coming from ambition or excellence, it was coming from a deep belief that nothing I did was ever enough. It's called 'unrelenting standards' and they're not about excellence, they're about proving you're worthy.

What I didn't know then was that my good little girl survival strategy had become my cycle. No-one tells you the thing about impossibly high standards — they're never high enough. There's always another gold star to earn, another promotion to chase, another way to prove you're worth keeping around.

The little voice that whispered *keep being better, push harder* wasn't intuition, this was what psychologists call an *unrelenting standards schema in action*. The voice wasn't asking me to be excellent because I was naturally ambitious, it was demanding perfection because my nervous system had learned that anything less than exceptional meant I wasn't safe.

Here's what happens when your beliefs run the show: Beliefs don't just sit in your mind, they become *patterns of behaviour* on repeat, your learned automatic responses to how you show up.

You don't just set high goals, you make your worth dependent on meeting them. You don't just work hard, you go beyond what is reasonable and sacrifice rest, relationships and anything that doesn't feed the achievement machine. These become your default.

I thought I was driven by ambition. Really, I was driven by the belief that I had to earn my place at the table every single day. I didn't realise these beliefs were driving my patterns. I never thought to question them. I just thought that was what you did to achieve.

Jeffrey Young's research[6] on early maladaptive schemas identifies the unrelenting standards schema as one of the most common patterns in high achievers: a belief that you must strive to meet very high internalised standards, a belief usually developed in childhood through conditional approval. When I interpreted Dad's attention as conditional on performance, my developing brain learned a simple equation: perfect performance = love and safety.

Studies show that perfectionist thinking activates the same neural pathways as trauma responses — your brain literally perceives 'not being the best' as a threat to survival. When I received feedback that wasn't glowing praise, when I made a mistake, when someone else got recognition I wanted, my brain didn't just feel disappointed. It felt like I was in actual danger.

Your unrelenting standards aren't a character flaw, they're a survival strategy your brilliant brain developed to keep you safe and feel loved. That little voice whispering 'push harder' isn't your enemy, it's a scared child who learned that perfect performance equals love and safety.

The problem isn't your standards, it's the unrelenting nature of them. When 95 per cent feels like failure instead of excellence, when no achievement ever feels good enough because the standard was unreachable from the start — that's not ambition, that's survival dressed up as success.

This relentless pursuit leads to what I call swanning behaviour.

Behaviour pattern 2: Swanning while drowning

When I was seven years old, I was a tap dancer. I had a big concert performance where my friend Jackie and I would be doing the tap dance routine *Hello, Dolly!* It was a big event for me as both my parents were showing up to see the performance. My dad often missed key moments of my life due to his work commitments so, for me, I really was so excited to perform.

My nerves hit the moment I peered out to see my parents waiting. I stepped onto stage and completely blanked — every rehearsed move vanished. I kept my well-practised smile on my face as if nothing had happened, and, while I was out of step for the entire routine, I pretended nothing was wrong. I finished the dance routine and Jackie was not happy with me. It was an utter disaster, and I wanted to crawl into a ball and hide from the world.

My parents forced out words of praise after the dance, yet I was devastated. Somehow, I thought my Dad would not love me now.

In that moment, I learned that love felt conditional: earned through perfect performance, lost through visible failure. I didn't realise this would become my life's operating system. Years later, I'd perfect this art of graceful swanning while drowning. What started as a seven-year-old's survival mechanism became my professional superpower. I became trapped in this endless loop of being overly capable, pushing myself to perform beyond what anyone actually expected while paddling like crazy underneath hoping no-one would notice.

The sleepless nights, the fear of failure, the hard work, the outstanding performances and over-delivering became my way of being. By the time I reached senior leadership, my swan act was flawless — and exhausting. As I progressed in my career, and was promoted ahead of the curve, I would dress the part too. Even though I was often the youngest in the room, I would 'power suit up' to look professional. I would groom myself to look attractive as attractive people are seen to be more successful. I would clomp around all day in excruciating high heels so I was tall and swan-like (always graceful yet powerful). I made it all look effortless so no-one could see the padding underneath.

Performing like a swan on the surface, but paddling like hell underneath where no-one could see.

Before every big meeting I would be a bundle of nerves, work myself hard to prepare, and then show up as if I was born to do this and had zero self-doubt. Moments before I had been questioning myself, fearing failure and feeling physically sick knowing that, for this next 'performance', I could forget my moves and be found out.

The more senior I became, the better I got at disguising my paddling and pretending. 'Fake it until you make it' became my new mantra.

I never really believed I was the graceful swan but I hoped I seemed like one on the outside: a well-dressed, put together leader who did everything beautifully and gracefully.

No-one other than me knew the real hidden cost of swanning. I became a prisoner of being overly capable, over performing and making it look effortless yet exhausting myself in maintaining the swan-like performance. The belief driving this pattern of behaviour was people-pleasing.

The science of swanning

Carl Jung's research into the persona[7] (what he called 'the compromise between the individual and society') explains the psychological foundation of swan behaviour. His work distinguishes between persona (the social mask, such as titles, roles, professional identity) and authentic self (the integrated personality, including both conscious and unconscious aspects).

Christina Maslach's pioneering research[8] identifies three distinct patterns that overachievers fall into: emotional exhaustion (the swan's paddling), depersonalisation (the swan's mask), and reduced personal accomplishment (the swan's empty victory). Research on professional identity formation shows that leaders often develop what researchers call 'provisional professional selves': performance-oriented identities that prioritise external validation over authentic self-expression.[9]

When we're constantly performing, we activate external validation circuits rather than intrinsic satisfaction pathways, creating disconnection from our authentic experience.

Any of this sound familiar? Do you swan?

The composure you maintain isn't performing gracefully while paddling like crazy, it's survival. You learned early that competence was currency and struggling wasn't allowed. You're not being fake, you're protecting yourself and others from the reality that high performance has a cost. The swan metaphor exists because it's universally true: Grace under pressure requires enormous hidden effort.

Your exhaustion isn't from being inauthentic, it's from the cognitive load of constant curation. Your desire to 'do it right' extended to living your life, turning even precious moments into another task to execute perfectly. You weren't disconnected by nature, you learned that how things look matter for survival and success. And so you overachieved in extraordinary ways, making it look effortless while working so hard to get there and sacrificing yourself along the way.

Behaviour pattern 3: Inner deal-making

Listen to yourself for 'just' one day. You'll be shocked how often that four-letter word slips out. Psychologists call this minimising language, and it's one of the most common patterns in people who struggle with boundaries.

Such a small word. Four letters that carry so much weight. We say it all the time without even realising.

- I just need to get through this week.
- I'll just rest when this project is done.
- I'll just push through today as needs must.
- Just one more email.
- Just this meeting, then I'm done.

It was only last week that I found myself back using the word 'just'. A client needed me to amend 160 slides and I fell into my overachiever ways. I got up at 5 am and worked solidly all day with minimal breaks. I had told my husband that I didn't have time to stop for dinner as I *just* needed to complete this deck.

No-one had asked for this deck to be done by the morning. I had set my own deadline and decided I would *just* push through and get it done so I could focus on my other priorities. That's when it hit me: I wasn't managing my workload, I was negotiating with myself like a hostage trying to appease a captor — and it was on me.

'Just' had become my unconscious self-abandonment strategy. It was so sophisticated I didn't even realise I was doing it. It was a default response whenever I needed to get shit done or achieve beyond my limits. I made it feel reasonable by prefacing everything with the word 'just' as part of the deal. It bypassed any reasonable thought and warning signals that my body and mind sent.

The truth is, 'just' became my internal deal-maker: the voice that convinced me to trade my wellbeing and what mattered to me for everyone else's needs, my delivery for their approval, my boundaries for their convenience. One small compromise at a time.

'Just' was my silent contract with proving. A tiny promise that relief or space or rest is just around the corner. A linguistic permission slip that makes the unreasonable sound achievable, the unmanageable feel manageable, the unreachable feel reachable. I spent many years negotiating with myself like this. Making inner deals. My 'just' deals were patterns of behaviour that served my need to prove constantly. Promising future relief in exchange for present sacrifice.

'Just' another shortcut

Understanding how 'just' works is one thing, seeing how it systematically destroys your protective systems is another. Research in linguistic psychology[10] reveals that our brains process minimising language differently than direct language. When we say 'I'll just work late' versus 'I'm just choosing to sacrifice my evening', we activate different neural pathways. The minimising language literally bypasses the circuits that would normally protect us from harmful choices.

No wonder 'just' felt so soothing, it was anaesthetising my survival instincts.

Dr. Roy Baumeister's research[11] reveals why 'just' becomes irresistible when we're overwhelmed: Our brains take shortcuts, and the shortest shortcut is always sacrificing ourselves.

What psychologists Henry Cloud and John Townsend[12] discovered about boundary erosion also follows a predictable pattern, and it's exactly what I lived through. 'Just' doesn't just manage your time, it dismantles your boundaries. They describe boundaries like a fence — every 'just this once' is like leaving the front door wide open.

And over time, I just surrendered to whatever was needed of me. I would always say 'yes' and figure out how to make it happen later. I was always the one staying late to get my real work done after everyone else had gone home, because I'd spent the day responding to urgent demands. I lost sight of what my needs even were, so I had very few boundaries, and my family resigned themselves to me being around as a bonus rather than a given. Work always came first, family and me last. With that one word, my boundaries didn't just erode, they evaporated. Each compromise made the next compromise easier until I was in complete freefall.

These deals aren't weakness, they're evidence of your optimism and problem-solving nature. You believe in solutions and possibilities. The issue isn't that you make these agreements, it's that you're consistently overestimating your future capacity while underestimating your current limits. Your brain is trying to resolve the conflict between what you want to do and what you can actually sustain.

You weren't being flexible, adaptable and capable. You were training yourself to believe your needs didn't matter, that your limits were suggestions, not requirements. Your denial isn't ignorance, it's determination mixed with terror.

Power pause: Another kind of '*just*'

Here's the plot twist that changed everything for me: The word that was my enemy could become my ally. Take a moment to think about how you could reframe 'just'.

What if we could reframe 'just' from self-abandonment to self-advocacy? What if this word could work for you instead of against you?

There's another kind of 'just', one that recognises your limits, honours your humanity and shows up for you when old patterns try to resurface:

Just let it go.

Just do you.

Just show up—that's enough.

Just take a break.

Just rest.

Just be.

Just breathe.

Just do this one thing and no more.

Just take a moment.

This 'just' allows you to hold boundaries, focus on what matters and prioritise authentically. This 'just' knows you're ambitious and human. This 'just' calls it rather than negotiates it away.

Using this word this way allows you to build trust with yourself by honouring small commitments to your own wellbeing and treating your needs as non-negotiables. Because that's what they are—not suggestions, not luxuries, not things to be earned. Your body speaks to you constantly about what it needs and it deserves to be heard. Ponder on that for a moment and consider how different your behaviour would be as a result.

Behaviour pattern 4: Pushing through

As a child of divorced parents, I didn't see my father often. He would make promises to see me and often not show as he was always busy doing a deal. So, from an early age, one of my core values was showing up no matter what. I was the person who never made a promise I couldn't keep. I called this integrity, and it built me tremendous respect with clients, bosses, teams and friends. I was the person they could count on to come through.

I often did this at the cost of me. I showed up no matter what and was the dependable one who always delivered. I didn't really think about what it meant to show up for myself. I was giving all of myself to everyone else because I knew too well the heartbreak of abandonment. This became one of my superpowers. I became known as the strong one, the resilient one. No matter the challenge or enormity of pressure, I endured and over-functioned beyond the norm. I even became known as 'the happy warrior'.

I was the perfect employee who took on more than my contracted hours, pushed through, delivered beyond expectations, rarely took leave and worked from home when sick. The more I achieved, the more responsibilities I received. I told myself I loved what I did and didn't want to let anyone down. I was being driven by my belief that I needed to perform at all costs, resulting in me ignoring all the signs. Everyone depended on my willingness to sacrifice myself for the greater good, so I always showed up no matter what — even if it meant coughing up blood!

Chronic stress research[13] shows how prolonged activation of our stress-response system impairs prefrontal cortex function, which is why you can solve complex business problems but can't see you need to rest. McEwen's allostatic load research[14] reveals the biological cost of chronic stress performance, how our bodies accumulate wear and tear from constant override of natural signals.

Your body will tell you what your mind refuses to hear. When you're constantly pushing through and showing up for everyone, you become so skilled at overriding your internal signals that physical symptoms become background noise — just another obstacle to manage rather than urgent messages demanding attention. Pushing through isn't resilience when your body is breaking down, it's resistance to reality and a complete disregard for your own limits. True strength isn't ignoring every signal that something's wrong, it's having the courage to actually listen before your body forces you to stop.

Behaviour pattern 5: Refusing to see reality

The final behavioural pattern that shows up for us as overachievers is *denial*. Our ability to see what really is and to accept it rather than keep on pretending. The reason this chapter is so important is because before we can change for the better, we have to be able to look at ourselves in the mirror and accept how we are showing up. Are we pretending or pushing through in the hope that things will change or are we accepting our reality and our limits?

Once when I was in hospital, I turned my bed into a corner office complete with laptop, notebook, jacket over my gown and makeup applied. The machines beeped their disapproval, but I had emails to answer. The nurses shook their heads. I called it Tuesday.

Luckily, as I was immune compromised, I got my own corner office (aka hospital room) with a view. 'Brilliant, I could keep going despite being stuck here for the week', I thought. Best way to kill time rather than waste it just lying here, right? No distractions either!

For the first six years of being sick, I was in complete and utter denial. I did not want to believe I had worked myself sick. I believed, as an overachiever, I could cure myself or fix this incurable disease. After all, I'd fixed everything else in my life through sheer effort, right?

The deep truth was that I did not want to accept my reality, the reality that I would be limited in my ability to achieve now that I was stuck in a sick body. Rest felt like failure. My belief in pushing through resulted in me denying what was really happening.

If I am also completely honest with you, I didn't know what to do with myself. Rest was not a natural state of being for me, so I was completely unable to process having no meetings other than hospital treatments, long periods of time to rest, and no money to shop or do the things I would dream of when I was achieving and had no time. Nope, I was unwell, everything was an effort, I had no goals other than to stay alive and, yet, I told myself I needed to keep going to keep the roof over our heads. I didn't think to slow down too.

I decided to be a high-performing sick person. No challenge too small for me, right? What no-one tells you about overachievers is that we don't just fear failure, we fear irrelevance. Irrelevance feels like death, and denial is a much easier option to pursue.

What I discovered about denial is that it's not just about refusing to see reality. It's about seeing reality perfectly clearly in private moments, then choosing to ignore it because change feels more terrifying than self-destruction.

Deny, deny, deny

When reality threatens our identity, our minds become masterful storytellers spinning narratives that protect our sense of self, even when those stories are slowly destroying us. When overachievers face loss, illness or failure, our brains perceive it as an existential threat. Neuroscientists call this 'amygdala hijack', when our rational thinking goes offline exactly when we need it most.

Research shows[15] that when we're in this threat state, our brains default to familiar patterns rather than optimal ones. So even though working myself literally to death by denying my reality was clearly destructive, it felt safer than the unknown territory of actually resting and dealing with my reality.

The second force around my denial was the fear of dying. Terror management theory reveals something profound: our consciousness of mortality drives us to create 'immortality projects', achievements that help us feel like we'll outlast our physical existence.

Perhaps most insidiously, chronic stress was affecting my ability to think clearly. I was in constant fight-or-flight mode, but because I'm intelligent and articulate, I became incredibly skilled at rationalising my destructive choices. Studies on emotional suppression reveal that when we consistently push down our authentic responses, it depletes our cognitive resources. It was simply too much to deal with, so denial became my default response.

Perhaps you're reading this and thinking that your situation is different. You are not sick. You are aware of your costs. But perhaps you wonder if, underneath, denial is your master. If you are saying any of the following to yourself, it could be a sign you are living in denial:

- My situation is different; I really don't have a choice.
- Once I get through this busy period, things will calm down.
- I'm not like those other overachievers. I actually enjoy my work.
- My family/team/company really needs me to be this available.
- I'll slow down when I hit [specific goal/age/achievement].
- This is just what success requires; everyone at my level works like this.

Here's the truth: every person who's ever hit a breaking point has said these exact words. Your denial isn't special. It's not more justified. It's just more articulate. I know because I said every single one of these things too. And I believed them completely — right up until my body forced me to face reality.

You've been conditioned to see acknowledgment of your limits as weakness rather than wisdom. The 'I'm fine' response protected you from well-meaning advice you didn't have capacity to implement and from the fear that admitting struggle would derail your carefully constructed success.

The compound effect

These patterns don't exist in isolation, they compound and feed each other. Your patterns work together, each strengthening the next. Unrelenting standards create the need for swanning. Swanning requires inner deal-making. Deal-making demands performing. Performing necessitates denial.

When autopilot takes over, you become a high-functioning zombie. You look successful from the outside, but inside you're operating like a computer with 20 tabs open, running on 2 per cent battery, about to crash. The real cost isn't exhaustion, it's erasure. You slowly disappear inside your own life, becoming a character you're playing rather than a human being.

What I know to be true

✧ You're not choosing these patterns, they're choosing you. Every time. They are running in the background like malware, making decisions before you even realise there's a choice. You think that you're being strong, capable and reliable, but really, you're acting out beliefs that no longer fit who you're becoming.

✧ The exhaustion isn't from doing too much, it's from performing constantly. Negotiating away your needs one 'just' at a time. Never letting anyone see the cost. That's not strength—it's sophisticated suffering.

✧ Your patterns are messengers. The swanning is signalling unrealistic standards. The 'just' is revealing self-abandonment. The pushing through is showing you where you don't trust you're already enough. Listen to what they're trying to tell you.

✧ When you start catching these patterns—naming them, interrupting them, choosing differently—something profound happens. You stop being run by invisible forces. You start responding rather than reacting. You create space between who you've been and who you're becoming.

✧ Every time you catch a pattern, you weaken its grip. Every time you choose differently, you strengthen a new neural pathway. Pattern by pattern, you reclaim your life.

Power pause: Your pattern inventory

Now that you've seen all five patterns, let's get specific about which ones are running your life. The ones you have on rinse and repeat.

What are the behaviours that you default to when under pressure?

▸ Perhaps you go above and beyond because your high, unrelenting standards make 95 per cent feel like failure?

▸ Are you swanning, pretending everything is fine when you are paddling like crazy underneath?

(continued)

> ‣ Making inner deals that sacrifice your needs promising to yourself 'just this once'?
> ‣ Maybe it's when you are the happy warrior performing above all else?
> ‣ Or perhaps you are in denial about your limits and keep pushing when your body says stop?
>
> Notice what comes up for you as you step back and think about how your beliefs are driving your patterns of behaviour. Now that you can see them clearly, you can begin to choose differently. The question isn't whether you recognise yourself here (you do), but which pattern is costing you the most right now, and whether you're ready to try a different way.
>
> Try this at the end of each day this week. Ask yourself:
>
> ‣ Which behaviour pattern showed up most today?
> ‣ What would I do differently if I trusted I was already enough?
> ‣ How can I hold tomorrow a little lighter?
> ‣ Just notice what comes up for you. Remember to be kind to yourself as you ask these questions.

Power pause: The 3 Ns practice

I'm going to ask you to try something else this week—and, yes, I know you're busy, but this will take less time than your morning coffee.

- *Notice:* Jot down one moment each day when your behaviour patterns feel like they're crushing you rather than lifting you up.
- *Name:* Give that behaviour pattern a name. For me, it is always over-pushing beyond my limits (I call her 'Penny the Pusher'; yours might be different).
- *New story:* Write yourself one kinder alternative, the kind of thing you'd say to your best friend; for example, 'Thanks Penny, I have done enough already today'.

Then sit with this: What has this behavioural pattern actually cost me? What might I discover if I held it just a little more lightly? Do this often enough, and you start training your nervous system to respond with compassion instead of criticism.

✧ Glittering truths ✧

If you only remember three things from this chapter, make them these:

1. Your patterns are your beliefs in action

Unrelenting standards, swanning while drowning, the endless 'just' negotiations, performing through exhaustion: These aren't random behaviours, they're precise manifestations of what you believe about your worth. Every pattern is a belief made visible. Once you see the connection, you can't unsee it.

2. These patterns once protected you, now they're keeping you stuck

Perfectionism kept you safe from criticism. People-pleasing earned connection. Pushing through got you promoted. But protection mechanisms that never switch off become prisons. The swanning that once impressed now isolates. The 'just' that seemed reasonable now erases your boundaries. What saved you is now slowly destroying you.

3. Awareness creates choice where there was only autopilot

When you catch yourself mid-swan, mid-'just', mid-performance, you create a pause. A moment where you can ask: 'Is this pattern serving me or costing me?' That pause is everything. It's where you reclaim agency over behaviours that have been running you.

<u>4</u>

CYCLE STAGE 3: THE SILENT COSTS

What got you here may be silently breaking you

> 'A woman is like a tea bag—you can't tell how strong she is until you put her in hot water.'
>
> —*Eleanor Roosevelt*

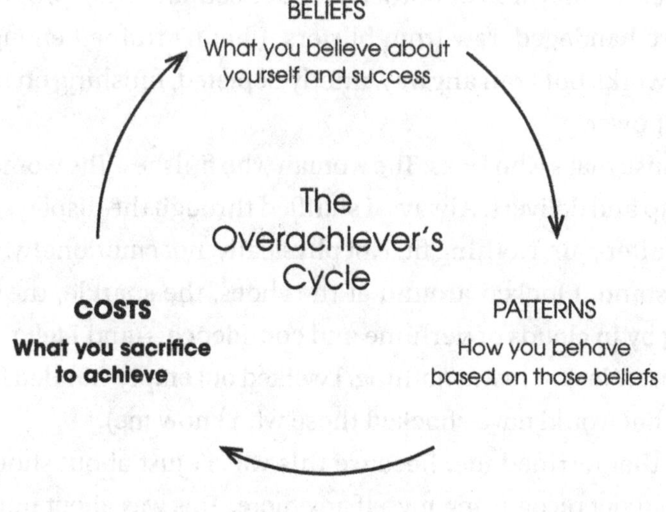

These patterns of behaviour don't stay sustainable. They create costs you don't see accumulating: physical exhaustion disguised as dedication, relationships that feel transactional, a gnawing sense that you're succeeding at everything except the life you're actually living. You know what it feels like to be achieving more while enjoying it less, proving your worth to everyone but yourself, running so fast you can't feel what's breaking until it's already broken.

What began as your greatest strengths — your drive, your standards, your excellence, your resilience — has become what's quietly depleting you. These costs feel gradual, almost manageable, until suddenly they're not. Until something forces you to stop.

Running on empty

I was in Paris, standing in Galeries Lafayette, on the shoe floor, specifically (my temple of joy). I mean who doesn't love shopping for shoes in Paris?

Rows of heels were displayed like art. I had come to celebrate, to reward myself for another finish line crossed: a 42-kilometre marathon through the vineyards of Bordeaux. But I couldn't walk properly. My feet were bandaged, raw from blisters. I hadn't trained enough (too busy at work), but I ran anyway, utterly depleted, finishing on nothing but willpower.

Because that's who I was: The woman who finishes. The woman who shows up and delivers. Always. I shuffled through the displays, trying on pair after pair. Nothing fit. Not physically, not emotionally. I could hardly stand. I looked around at the shoes, the sparkle, the people floating by in clouds of perfume and confidence — and I felt nothing. Not desire. Not joy. Just... nothing. I walked out empty-handed (a rarity for me that would have shocked those who know me).

And that terrified me. Because this wasn't just about shoes. This was about not recognising myself any more. This was about numbness seeping in where there used to be certainty. I was in Paris, in my happy place, and I couldn't find a single thing that made me feel alive.

Something was deeply wrong. It had been wrong for a long time.

Sure the signs were there: the fatigue that no amount of sleep could fix, breathlessness, the quiet ache in my bones. My body was shouting, and I chose to ignore the signs.

Then came Bordeaux. Forty-two kilometres of grit and denial. At kilometre 22, I started coughing. It wasn't a tickle, it was a deep, tearing, violent hack. By the end of the race, I was coughing blood. But I didn't stop. Of course, I didn't. I finished. Because finishers don't quit. Because achievers don't stop. Because I had taught myself to ignore everything my body tried to say. Until my body forced me to listen.

Back home, the scans confirmed what I had refused to see: sarcoidosis. Stage 4. Incurable. And, just like that, the world I had built—the one held up by grit, persistence, pushing through no matter what—it all began to collapse.

This was the moment for me where I began to question whether my definition of success had cost me too much. The short answer? *Yes*. I was trapped in a sick body with an incurable disease, not sure if I would make it to my 40th birthday and watching my success disappear. I felt totally out of control as to what was next. I wondered if I had finally pushed myself too far, having ignored all the signs, and worked myself to death with no way out. Perhaps I wasn't invincible after all.

The silent costs of overachieving

There are five common silent costs I see consistently with overachievers. You may be aware your achievement is costing you. Or you're so busy achieving you don't have the time to consider the cost. Or perhaps, like me, you're choosing to ignore all the signs even when they're shouting at you.

Silent cost #1: Emotional numbness (anhedonia)

When achievement feels hollow.

At the beginning of my career, every win was a triumph. I celebrated for days. It filled my soul. But as overachievement became the norm, the wins felt smaller. I'd achieve the goal, then immediately chase the next thing. No celebration. No pause. Just onto the next hit. I was addicted to the chase, not the achievement. And by the time I got there, I was too exhausted to feel anything.

Maybe this is you. Constantly onto the next achievement, never standing still, always hunting for the next dopamine spike. You're winning. But you can't feel it any more.

Silent cost #2: Decision fatigue

When simple choices become overwhelming.

I remember hearing the story of an emergency doctor who finished a double shift, making life-changing decisions all night long. She stops at the supermarket for cereal. Standing in the aisle, staring at Coco Pops and Froot Loops, she breaks down. She can't choose. Can't move. Her mind has shut down.

That's decision fatigue.

For me, it's when I can't decide what to wear in the morning, a sign I'm beyond exhausted. The simplest decisions become unclear.

As overachievers, we think we can make decision after decision, day after day, without rest or reflection. That we can retain the same clarity indefinitely. We can't.

Intensive decision making depletes your brain's energy resources. Your decision quality deteriorates throughout the day. That moment when you snap at someone after a marathon meeting day? Your prefrontal cortex has run out of fuel.

Silent cost #3: Relationship erosion

When everyone gets the leftover version of you.

I'm guilty of this one. I'd give myself to everyone all day, then drive home wiped out, barely able to hold a conversation with my loved ones. I just wanted TV to wash over me. I had nothing left.

You're physically present but mentally absent at celebrations, for important conversations, at school concerts. Your friend repeats what they just said because your mind drifted to a work challenge. Conversations become transactional, not connective. You're there, but you're not really there.

Silent cost #4: Identity crisis

When you don't know who you are without the achieving.

You meet someone new. The first thing out of your mouth? Your role. Not your name. Not who you are, what you do. When someone asks how you are, you tell them what you're doing, not how you're feeling. Doing nothing for a day feels terrifying. Rest feels like failure.

When I had to step away from work for treatment, I asked my therapist: 'What could I achieve during these five months?' She said, 'How about just navigating treatment and staying well?' My sense of worth was so fused with achievement that simply staying alive didn't feel like enough. I'd forgotten how to just be.

Psychologists call this 'identity fusion', when you become so merged with your role that you can't separate who you are from what you do. Studies show that high achievers are particularly vulnerable because their self-worth is tied directly to output.

Silent cost #5: Future anxiety

When you're terrified of slowing down.

The thought of slowing down feels unthinkable. If you stop, everything will fall apart. You'll fail. Be found out. Worse — all the sacrifice will have been for nothing.

Rest, for me, felt like death. Even when my body was shouting at me to stop, I couldn't. Even facing a chronic illness, I became a high-performing sick person. I kept going, kept pushing and achieving for fear of slowing down.

Research shows high achievers often use goal-setting and achievement as a coping mechanism,[16] a way to avoid uncomfortable emotions or distress. The brain's reward system creates a dopamine response to achievement[17] that can become self-reinforcing. Rest feels dangerous because it threatens the momentum that feels like proof of worth.

You believe if you stop pushing, everything collapses. So you simply don't stop.

Power pause: Your silent cost counter

Before we go deeper, take a moment to reflect on these silent costs. Really dig deeper here, be honest with yourself, and ask:

▸ Which of these five costs resonates most strongly with you right now? Or is there another one sitting silently within you that has surfaced?

▸ What part of yourself have you lost in the pursuit of success?

▸ If you continue on this path for another year, what will you lose that you can't get back? What are you prepared to sacrifice to get there? At what point will it be too much or too late? When will the cost be too high?

Be honest. No-one's watching. This is just you, taking inventory of what your current pace is actually costing you.

A dangerous place to be

What makes this so dangerous for leaders like us is that your brain can't distinguish between a genuine emergency and your packed calendar. It treats every deadline like a life-or-death situation.

According to Selye's groundbreaking research[18] from the 1930s (yes, the 1930s), your body has three predictable responses to prolonged stress: alarm, resistance and exhaustion. Most high performers live permanently in the 'resistance' phase, where your body pumps out stress hormones like cortisol and adrenaline to keep you functioning at unsustainable levels. What Selye discovered was chilling: this phase always ends the same way—with complete system breakdown.

You're running your nervous system like you're running a marathon in heels, telling yourself you'll be fine, that you've done harder things, wondering why your feet are bleeding and you can't remember why you're still running.

And it's the small costs that compound. That one school concert. That one decision made in haste. That one late night. That one extra thing you take on. We minimise it. We believe it's worth it. Until 'I'm just tired' becomes 'I'm never not tired'. Until that extra thing becomes too many things. Until 'it's just a cough' becomes a chronic illness where you wish you could reverse time.

I ignored all the smaller costs to pursue my definition of success, which vanished overnight when I had to fight to stay alive.

Why 'temporary sacrifice' never ends

I truly believed my sacrifices were temporary. That once I got 'there', I'd be able to enjoy it more. If I worked 80-hour weeks and exceeded every expectation, I'd eventually have more balance. If I achieved my goals, I could take a break. After this big project, things would get easier. I thought I was invincible. That all these sacrifices were worth it.

Until they weren't.

Then I started getting curious about what was really happening, why I couldn't seem to stop or even slow down even when I knew the pace was unsustainable. I discovered our brains become chemically dependent on achievement. We get stuck in a dopamine-driven loop where the hit of accomplishment creates a cycle of rationalisation. The sacrifice feels 'worth it' because we're externally validated. So we keep looking for the next goal to get the next hit.

Reading this research, I finally understood why I felt like I was going crazy. I wasn't weak or broken, I was experiencing withdrawal from my achievement drug. Your brain's reward system (the mesolimbic pathway) releases dopamine when you accomplish something. This circuit drives motivation by signalling that your actions are worth repeating. But when this system becomes overstimulated, your brain adapts. Normal rewards lose their impact. You need escalating achievements just to feel the same satisfaction.

This is why that promotion you worked yourself to the bone for felt flat within a week. Why hitting your revenue target didn't bring the joy you expected. Why you're already chasing the next thing before you've even celebrated this thing.

And it gets worse.

Research shows that high-achieving perfectionists don't just think differently, they experience stress differently.[19] Their stress-response system becomes chronically activated, keeping them in a persistent state of heightened arousal.[20] Over time, this elevated stress baseline becomes normalised in the body and brain.

You're literally living in chronic stress activation, but your brain has adapted to this as 'normal', so you can't even recognise how depleted you are. Think back to silent cost #1 on page 56 where I talked about 'incentive sensitisation', when the craving to achieve grows stronger, but the joy of achieving weakens. You need bigger wins, more accolades, greater output to feel anything at all. Eventually, even success feels flat.

This is why the wins stopped feeling like wins for me. Why I'd achieve my goals and immediately move on. Why nothing was ever enough. My reward system had become dysregulated. I was chasing a high that my brain could no longer deliver.

Remember the patterns from Chapter 3? The perfectionism, the people-pleasing, the optimism that keeps you pushing? They're not just behaviours, they're the very mechanisms that blind you to these warning signs. You interpret exhaustion as evidence you need better systems. You see emotional numbness as proof you need to focus harder. You explain away relationship erosion as temporary sacrifice. And so The Overachiever's Cycle continues.

In short, your coping mechanisms have become your blind spot. You already know when the costs are happening. You've known for a while. The exhaustion that sleep doesn't fix. The moment your partner asked if you're okay and you snapped. You told yourself this feeling is temporary. It'll get better after this project. After the promotion. After things slow down. Or when I get to my holiday.

But things never slow down, though, do they?

Your body's desperate SOS

Christina Maslach's research[21] found that burnout progresses through three predictable stages: emotional exhaustion, depersonalisation and reduced personal accomplishment.

Overachiever's translation: Feeling depleted every day. Reacting vs responding day in day out. Working harder but feeling less effective.

Or, here's the kicker… what normally takes you five minutes is now taking forever. Sound familiar?

These are biological warnings. Bruce McEwen's research found that your body accumulates damage from never switching off and always being 'on', such as elevated blood pressure, disrupted sleep, compromised immune function and cognitive decline.[22]

The hardest part? You interpret the symptoms that should make you stop (fatigue, brain fog, irritability) as evidence that you need to push harder. I chose to ignore the signs when my body was literally shouting at me, and perhaps the same is true for you right now.

There were many red flags as a result of my patterns of behaviour. In fact, they were painted loudly on a neon sign for me to see, but I chose to pretend they were not there.

Here are the three red flags that are the true costs of the overachiever's cycle:

- *Physical:* your body's alarm bells (Table 4.1)
- *Emotional:* your feelings flatline (Table 4.2)
- *Relational:* everyone gets the leftover version of you (Table 4.3, overleaf).

You don't need all three to be in trouble. One is enough.

These red flags progress through three stages:

1. early warnings you ignore
2. mid-stage alerts you rationalise
3. late-stage signals that force you to stop.

Table 4.1 Red flag #1: Physical

Physical red flags	Your body's alarm signals
Early warning	• You wake up already exhausted. • You need caffeine to function. • Your jaw is clenched and your tummy is doing somersaults by 10 am. • You're getting sick more often. • You're making silly small mistakes. • Your body aches for no reason.
Mid-stage	• Sleep doesn't restore you any more: you haven't had a good night's sleep in forever. • Your heart races lying in bed and you wake up at 3 am most nights ruminating. • Headaches won't quit and you simply can't think clearly. • Your digestion is a mess: you are comfort eating, skipping meals or numbing with alcohol. • You gained (or lost) weight without trying.
Late stage	• You're in physical pain. • You got a diagnosis you can't ignore. • Your immune system has collapsed. • Your body literally stopped you.

Table 4.2 Red flag #2: Emotional

Emotional red flags	When your emotions flatline
Early warning	• The wins feel smaller or less satisfying. • You snap over nothing. • Anxiety shows up unexpectedly. • Sunday night dread is intensifying. • You can't remember the last time you felt excited or joy.

(continued)

Table 4.2 Red flag #2: Emotional (*cont'd*)

Emotional red flags	When your emotions flatline
Mid-stage	• Nothing really moves you any more. • You're desensitised when someone tells you something upsetting. • You've become cynical about everything or frustrated with everyone. • You're detached from your own life. • Joy and contentment feel foreign. • You're just going through the motions.
Late stage	• Complete emotional shutdown — you're numb. • You question why any of it matters. • Everything feels meaningless. • You fantasise about escaping or running away. • You have dark thoughts you don't tell anyone. • You crave relief and wish you could become a florist or Uber driver.

Table 4.3 Red flag #3: Relational

Relational red flags	Everyone gets the leftover version of you
Early warning	• You cancel plans with loved ones because you're too tired. • You're on your phone during family dinner. • Your friend said you seem stressed or always tired. • Your partner asked if you're okay and you said 'fine'. • You were physically there but mentally absent.
Mid-stage	• Conversations feel like tasks. • You avoid social situations entirely as you don't have the energy. • Your family stopped expecting you to show up as you are always too busy. • You prefer to be alone — it's easier. • The people closest to you feel like strangers as they don't get your world. • It's been a long time since you had a laugh or fun.

Relational red flags	Everyone gets the leftover version of you
Late stage	• Complete withdrawal. • You can't connect even when you try. • Relationships have become hollow or transactional. • You feel profound isolation while surrounded by people. • You've forgotten what connection feels like. • All work, no play.

What I know to be true

✧ Every overachiever has a breaking point. Every single one. The only variable is when and how spectacularly it arrives. You're a human running on an operating system that demands you to be superhuman.

✧ The silent costs (emotional numbness, decision fatigue, relationship erosion, identity crisis, future anxiety) aren't side effects, they're the main event.

✧ You already know something's not right. That's why you're reading this. You've felt it. Your body knows. Your relationships know. Deep down, you know.

✧ The challenge isn't that you might break, it's that you think breaking is failure. Sometimes what looks like falling apart is actually where your greatest growth comes.

Here's the invitation: Reset now, while it's still your choice. Listen to the whispers before they become screams. Choose to change before change chooses you.

Because there's another way to achieve, to lead, to live. One that doesn't require you to sacrifice everything that matters on the altar of success.

Power pause: Your red flags

When you look at tables 4.1–4.3, which ones do you tick off the most? What stage do you think you are in right now for each of them?

I ignored every warning sign. Every single one. I told myself I was strong, resilient, built for this. I was wrong. By the time I had no choice, I was in a hospital bed wondering if I'd see my kids grow up.

You have a choice right now. You can catch this now when it's exhaustion and overwhelm, or you can wait until your body forces you to stop. The warning signs aren't there to scare you, they're there to save you. Every overachiever has a breaking point as you are only human.

The question is whether you'll listen before you reach it.

Recognising these costs, checking those boxes, seeing yourself in these red flags—that's not the reset. That's just finally admitting there's a cost to the way you achieve.

Power pause: Non-negotiables declaration

Before we move to Part II, pause here. Think of one thing you've lost about yourself that you want back. Not miss…want back. Missing keeps you stuck. Wanting it back? That's where change begins. For me, I missed my playfulness and laughter as I had become too serious in the pursuit of success.

Think back to before the relentless achieving took over:

▸ What have you abandoned that made you feel alive?

▸ What brought you joy that you've sacrificed for achievement?

> ▸ If you could reclaim one part of yourself tomorrow, what would it be?

Write it down. This isn't nostalgia, it's your north star for who you're becoming. And here's your challenge: Do one small thing to reclaim it today. Not tomorrow. Today.

Your non-negotiables

Based on everything you've recognised in this chapter, identify three things you will no longer sacrifice. Here are mine:

1. Every day I do one thing to fill my cup before the day takes over.
2. No work meetings before 9 am—my mornings are mine.
3. I plan my day every morning before checking emails: impact over inbox.

Now it's your turn. Write them somewhere you'll see them daily. Phone lock screen. Post-It note. Bathroom mirror. Laptop background. These aren't suggestions, they're your foundation for what comes next.

Part II is where the real inner work begins. The work ahead isn't about lowering your standards or abandoning your goals, it's about reshaping the operating system that's convinced you the only way to succeed is to run yourself into the ground.

You've seen the costs. You've recognised the warning signs. You know something has to change. Now it's time to understand why this keeps happening, and how to interrupt the cycle before your body makes the decision for you.

✨ Glittering truths ✨

If you only remember three things from this chapter, make them these:

1. The costs aren't theoretical, they're compounding daily

Physical exhaustion deepens emotional numbness. Emotional depletion destroys relationships. Relational disconnection accelerates everything. Your achievement is already costing you.

2. Your warning signs are wisdom, not failure

That exhaustion that sleep doesn't fix? That's data. The hollow feeling after achieving something huge? Information. The snap at someone you love? Intelligence. Your brain and body are sending signals to save you from yourself.

3. You can choose to reset now or be forced to stop later

The voluntary reset (where you consciously choose to change) is always gentler than the involuntary breakdown. You can listen to the whispers or wait for the scream. The choice is yours, but only for so long.

<u>PART II</u>

THE INNER RESET: REDEFINING SUCCESS INSIDE OUT

'We must be willing to let go of the life we planned so as to have the life that is waiting for us.'

—*Joseph Campbell*

It's an inside job

Part II is where the real reset begins... and that's with your inner narrative. The beliefs that drive you. The stories that shape you. And the bravery to challenge them, reframe them and create a better way to achieve — not at the cost of you.

There are three mindset shifts to address the core internal relationships keeping overachievers stuck:

1. *Your relationship with effort and worth:* the belief that you must constantly prove your value.
2. *Your relationship with identity and authenticity:* the performance masks you wear to be accepted.
3. *Your relationship with control and reality:* the exhausting grip on outcomes you can't actually control.

These aren't surface-level productivity hacks, they're the foundational beliefs that determine whether you achieve at the cost of yourself or create success that includes you.

All three are essential mindset resets before you can build a sustainable new way of leading and living in Part III.

The journey is sequential:

1. *First, you'll discover you're already enough.* Not when you achieve more. Not when you prove more. Right now. And that realisation will give you permission to stop the relentless chase once and for all.
2. *Then you'll reclaim who you actually are* underneath all the performing. Dropping the masks. The real, whole, honest you.
3. *Finally, you'll loosen your grip on control* and learn to accept what is, discovering that the only thing you can truly control is your response — and that's where real freedom lives.

These shifts don't make you less ambitious, they make you *sustainably* ambitious. They don't ask you to settle, they show you how to succeed without losing yourself in the process.

This is the inner work that changes everything.

So let's begin.

5

MINDSET RESET #1: ENOUGH ALREADY

You were always enough—the achievement just made it harder to see

> 'No-one can make you feel inferior without your consent.'
>
> —*Eleanor Roosevelt*

The blue two-piece suit

I walked into work on Monday morning in a beautiful blue two-piece suit.

Four days later, I was still wearing it.

No sleep. No shower. No change of clothes. Just me, that suit, some underarm deodorant and perfume, and the promise that this pitch would finally prove how exceptional I was.

I lost 3 kilos from sheer stress alone. My body literally consumed itself to fuel my pursuit of perfection. By Thursday, the suit hung differently. Looser. A physical reminder of what I was willing to sacrifice.

Finally, the big moment arrived…

I stood at that easel, holding each presentation board, simultaneously exhausted and exhilarated. All of my bosses' eyes were on me, and they were leaning in to make sure I delivered. Then it happened. Mid-presentation, my eyelids began closing every time I looked down. My sleep-deprived body was shutting down, but my mind screamed: 'Come on, get it together, this is it now.' I pushed through, delivering the presentation in a blur.

The moment it ended, I walked into the hotel foyer and collapsed on a couch. My body had simply… stopped.

We didn't win the business. My bosses praised my 'dedication', but I was broken for weeks. And still, my first thought wasn't 'this is unsustainable', it was 'What did I do wrong? Next time, I'll push even harder.'

No-one stepped in to help me realise that this was not the way to deliver a world-class pitch. The complete opposite. I never thought to take care of myself during that week of huge pressure and delivery. I never considered going home to change or eat or rest before the pitch moment. It felt non-negotiable.

This way of performing did not set me up for success, it set me up for a collapse. That's when I knew: I wasn't running towards success, I was running from the terror of not being enough. This was where the first crack of 'perhaps there's a better way' began to form, but I wasn't ready to see it yet.

Maybe your version wasn't a blue suit. Maybe it was the:

- promotion you worked yourself sick to earn
- all-nighter that became your badge of honour
- 'yes' you said when your body was screaming 'no'.

Whatever your blue suit moment was, you know the cost — and you know you can't keep paying it.

When exhaustion became excellence

That pitch wasn't an anomaly. It was my operating system.

The 'happy warrior', as I was affectionately named by the global CEO of Ogilvy, I was the one who could handle any crisis. Vodafail. Qantas rebrand. The unrealistic deadlines, the high-stakes moments, the clients everyone else feared.

I was the one who showed up, no matter what. And I wore it like armour.

My belief of 'have it all, do it all, be it all' sat behind every sacrifice. The more I efforted, the more I was praised. The more I was praised, the more I attached it to my identity. And so the loop continued:

Effort → Validation → Identity → More effort → Repeat

See if you recognise yourself here:

- You're praised for going above and beyond, so you do it again.
- Rest feels like laziness, so you push through.
- 'Just enough' feels dangerous, so you always do more.

This isn't excellence. I call it *efforting* — that relentless, exhausting cycle of endless trying, pushing, proving. It's more than working hard. It's the white-knuckle grip on achievement that never lets you rest, never lets you be enough. It's striving at a cost to you that is not sustainable.

The three stories that were destroying me

Here's what I believed for most of my life: Effort equals worth. The harder I worked, the more valuable I became. Rest was for people who didn't care about excellence. Saying 'no' meant I wasn't committed enough. And doing just enough? That was the same as failing.

I didn't know I was living three stories on repeat, stories I thought were facts about how the world worked. These weren't beliefs I'd consciously chosen, they were invisible scripts running my life, quietly exhausting me:

Story #1: I haven't done enough

If it's worth doing, it's worth doing extraordinarily.

Nothing I did ever felt good enough. That pitch I stayed up four nights preparing? The moment it was over, I was already thinking 'I should have done more.'

The promotion I worked years for felt hollow within days. The project I poured myself into got a 'well done', and I immediately thought 'I should have added more'.

I was always planning the next thing before celebrating the last thing. Standing still felt like falling behind. 'Just enough' felt like failure.

Every achievement evaporated the moment I completed it — not because they weren't significant, but because I'd told myself the story that nothing was ever complete, never excellent, never enough.

Story #2: I'm not enough

I need to prove I am worthy to feel enough.

Deep down, I didn't believe I was worthy as I was. No matter how brilliant my work, there was always room for improvement. If I wasn't working hard, I'd be found out as an imposter.

To feel worthy, I needed to show everyone how good I was — constantly. No off days. No mistakes. Always on, always performing, always proving to those who mattered how capable I was.

All while doubting myself every single day.

Just being me wasn't an option. It took work, polish and proving day in and day out. I couldn't just show up and trust that I was enough, I had to earn my place at the table over and over again.

Even when I was the most qualified person in the room, I was the one who felt like I didn't belong there.

Story #3: I don't have enough

I'll be enough when I finally have ________.

This story wasn't about achievements, it was the perpetual feeling that something essential was missing, that my definition of success was tied to some checklist of 'haves'. At the time I fell sick, I had it all. I was the definition of what I felt success was, yet I was still chasing more.

I was always one thing away from having enough:

- One more qualification and I'd finally feel credible.
- One more client turnaround and I'd finally feel secure.
- One more zero in the bank account and I'd finally relax.
- One more recognition and I'd finally feel enough.

Scarcity sat underneath everything: not enough time, not enough money, not enough experience, not enough proof that I belonged here.

I lived with a low-grade anxiety that I was operating from deficit. That everyone else had something I didn't. That I was always playing catch-up, always behind, always benchmarking myself to others, always lacking the one thing that would make me feel settled.

The scarcity mindset kept me running…not towards something, but away from the fear that I was fundamentally lacking and I needed evidence of 'haves' to prove it.

No amount of achieving, accumulating or advancing ever made that feeling go away. Because the problem wasn't what I didn't have, it was the story I was telling myself about not being enough without it.

These three stories fed each other and, together, they created an unrealistic standard I could never meet.

Which story is yours? You don't need to answer this question right now. Just notice which one made your chest tighten as you read it.

That's the one stealing your energy. That's the one we're going to rewrite.

Enough already, darling

I was catching up with Jo at a gorgeous beachfront cafe in Manly after two solid days of workshop delivery. I was exhausted but buzzing.

Jo had been my coach years earlier. She was the one who helped me leave corporate when I wanted to take my impact bigger. She knew the roles where I'd sacrificed my health. She'd seen my patterns before I had.

And sitting across from her that day, I was doing it again.

I was sharing the success of my latest leadership program, already moving to the next thing: my grand plans to scale bigger, reach more people, transform 10 000 leaders.

'I'm exhausted', I admitted, 'but I want to help 10 000 leaders. I want to take it bigger to make real impact now while I can.'

Jo looked at me with that knowing smile, the one that said *I see what you're doing.*

Then she said eight words that shattered everything: 'But darling, what if you've already done enough?'

The words hit me like lightning.

My chest tightened. My breath caught. I felt it in my body before my mind could process it, that particular cocktail of resistance and recognition that only truth brings.

I opened my mouth to argue, to list all the leaders I hadn't reached yet, all the impact I hadn't made, all the work left undone.

But nothing came out.

Because something in me knew: She was right.

That tension, between wanting to believe it and being terrified to stop proving, that's where the shift begins.

I was doing it again. Chasing. Proving. Desperately trying to earn my enoughness through bigger numbers, wider reach, more impact.

Despite rebuilding my life while being chronically ill. Despite everything I'd already overcome. Despite already having helped hundreds of leaders. Despite knowing better—I'd fallen straight back into my old pattern. My drive to achieve was still trying to prove I was worthy.

Then another thought bubbled up as I sat with the question. What if I was enough as I am and didn't need to prove my worth any more? How different would my life be?

I felt something shift in my body. A lightness. A release. Like I'd been holding my breath for decades and someone had finally given me permission to exhale.

Something deep inside me whispered: *You can stop now. You've done enough.*

So I explored this question for weeks: *What if I had already done enough?* I checked in on why I was pushing myself and still working so goddamn hard despite being in a sick body. I knew I needed to shift my mindset as this old one was not serving me any more, so I wrote down those words and put them on my desk so I could remind myself when I caught myself falling into efforting and proving.

I have already done enough.

I stepped back from the doing for a moment and looked at my career: the programs built, the leaders I had helped and transformed, the lives impacted as a result of my story and leadership programs. I realised that even helping one leader was enough.

I looked at my family: children who know they are loved, a partnership that had weathered storms, connection with my family.

I looked at my response to my illness: the courage I'd shown, the grace and resilience I'd found in facing my incurable illness, overcoming the challenges it presented and being able to rebuild my life despite it all.

In doing this, I realised that I'd dismissed every achievement the moment I achieved it, that I had just kept pushing, never letting anything land, never letting it be enough. And I needed to finally stop the chase and actually own that I had already done enough. Boom! Life liberating. Game changing. I gave myself permission to let go and sit with my enoughness.

It sounds simple now that I write it, but in that moment, letting myself acknowledge what I'd already created felt revolutionary.

This wasn't about stopping, it was about finally letting myself arrive.

I already was enough.

Then I sat with me and I realised that my worth wasn't actually conditional on my output. It had never been. Worth was inherent and known, not earned. I didn't need to prove, perform or perfect to deserve love, rest and belonging. I was no longer my achievements alone.

This one was harder for me to rewrite. Because 'doing enough' was external. I could list achievements, but 'being enough'? That required me to believe my worth wasn't earned.

Stripped of all my titles, roles, achievements … was I still worthy? My children said 'yes'. My partner said 'yes'. But could I say 'yes' to me?

The answer that emerged surprised me: I already was enough. I'd just been too busy proving it to notice. So I stepped into the deep knowing that I am imperfectly perfect as I am. I am enough.

I already had enough.

Having lost everything I had worked for when I got sick, I had already learned the lesson that I had enough. Home is where you make it, not what you have. I had learned to seek comfort in what I did have, not what I didn't. This one felt easier because I had already let go of the loss of losing my homes. As long as my family and friends were with me, I had enough. The rest was just stuff.

The time I have left on this planet is still mine to choose how I use it. That life didn't need to be perfect, and I had already learned that the only things you can really control are your breath and this moment. I just needed to remind myself of this inner truth as it was so easy for me to fall back into the chase of what I didn't have.

It was then I realised that enoughness isn't the end of excellence, it's the beginning of sustainable excellence. It's the difference between sprinting and marathon running. It's the moment you stop seeking your value in metrics external to you and start finding it in what's true to what you believe and how you feel inside. It's the clarity to know with certainty: I can still want more without needing more.

This life. This moment. This imperfect, uncertain, chronically ill, still-showing-up life. It was enough. Not because it was perfect. Not because I had everything I wanted. But because it was mine. And I was present for it.

When was the last time someone asked you: 'What if you've already done enough?'

Notice what comes up. Fear? Lightness? Both?

Owning your space

From that moment on, I saw my life differently. I let go of the performance and stood in my sense of self rather than efforting to be someone. I was simply me — already enough as I am, my imperfectly perfect self. I felt at ease, content with knowing I am enough as I am.

I owned my worth differently. It wasn't earned through sacrifice but by showing up prepared, ready and clear on the value I bring into any room. I owned my story, my capabilities, my smarts and knew I had earned my right to stand at the front of a room and be of genuine service to the leaders who were entrusting me to help them. I didn't need to collapse in another hotel foyer at the end of a workshop to prove my value.

I learned to prime and prepare myself to show up fully by resting the day before, by trusting I had what it took to deliver and, even when I wasn't sure or I was overwhelmed by the amazing room of talent, I leaned into my wobbles and showed up as me. In fact, I was in a room recently with 140 leaders from a beauty brand, feeling nervous and not 100 per cent well. Then I just said to myself: 'You've got this. Just do you.' And I did.

I also saw my future differently. I still didn't know what my health would be like, I still had to work and rebuild my future, I still wanted to show up fully to help leaders and live my best life. I trusted and consciously showed up every day from a place of enoughness. Tuning into what lights me up, letting go of what doesn't and making sure I am present to what is. Intentionally choosing to be content in the moment and not 'when I have X, then I'll be happy'. I fully appreciate how lucky I am every day I can get out of bed, put my feet on the floor and show up for what life has to offer.

Sarah's story: The juggle that almost broke her

When Sarah, a senior leader to 300 people, first came to me, she was completely exhausted. She had the sharp blazer, polished style (a fellow lover of sequins) and the kind of presence people noticed when she walked into a room. On paper? Thriving. In reality? Running on fumes.

Her new boss had unrelenting standards, the kind that pushed everyone to excellence. For every 100 things Sarah did brilliantly, the conversation focused on the one thing that could be improved. And because pleasing was her instinct, she worked even harder, trying to anticipate every need before it was spoken, to stay one step ahead of the high expectations.

On the outside, she had it all. She was the main income earner for her family, she had a partner she adored and a young child who lit up her world. She had the kind of life that looked impressive, balanced, successful.

But it was costing her everything.

The sleepless nights came first. Sarah would lie awake anticipating what was coming next, her mind racing through scenarios, preparing responses, trying to stay one step ahead.

Did I do enough? Was that the right call? Will they think I'm not capable?

She didn't want to let anyone down — not her clients, not her team, not the high standards she was being held to. So she worked harder. Responded faster. Prepared more thoroughly.

The extra glass of wine at night became her way to switch off, to numb the constant hum of 'not enough' that followed her home from work. She was chasing her life instead of living it, proving constantly that she was worthy of the role, the salary, the respect she desperately needed to feel.

As the main income earner, failure wasn't an option. Her family depended on her. That pressure compounded everything. The anxiety bled into home. She'd snap at her child over minor things. Sit with her partner while mentally drafting emails. Her boundaries eroded so gradually, she didn't notice until they were gone.

Despite performing at the highest level, despite exceeding expectations, she felt like she was failing.

When Sarah and I started working together, I asked her the same question that was put to me by my friend Jo:

'What if you're already enough? What if all this efforting isn't making you more valuable? Perhaps it's just exhausting you while you chase proof you don't need?'

The unspoken fear hung between us: *If I stop performing, they'll realise I'm not actually good enough.*

I gave her permission to do something radical. Slow down. Prioritise herself. Remember what actually mattered.

'Let go of the efforting', I told her. 'Fill your cup by taking care of yourself first. Not after you've proven yourself. First.'

Something started to shift.

Sarah started noticing the efforting she'd normalised. The obsessive preparation. The constant second-guessing. The volunteering for additional projects because saying 'no' felt like proof she couldn't handle it.

She began moving through her day with a different perspective: *I am enough. I have done enough. I don't need to prove my worth through exhausting performance.*

When feedback focused on what could be improved, instead of spiralling and working through the night to prove herself, Sarah took a breath. She assessed objectively: *Is this valid feedback? Or am I internalising these high standards?* She made the improvements that mattered and left the rest.

She felt lighter.

The sleepless nights eased. Not because the external pressure decreased, but because she stopped internalising it as proof she wasn't enough. She set boundaries without apologising. Showed up for her child without her mind being halfway in her inbox.

Her partner noticed first. 'You're more present. It's like I got you back.'

Sarah realised that she'd been so busy proving she was enough at work that she'd disappeared from her own life. The shift Sarah made was internal: accepting she was already enough, regardless of performance. That acceptance revealed the cost of staying in an environment that demanded constant proving was no longer acceptable.

'I wish I'd asked for help sooner', Sarah reflects. 'I wish I'd recognised the warning signs: the sleep issues, the drinking, the anxiety bleeding into home. I kept thinking the answer was to try harder. To prove more.'

What changed when I chose to believe it

It was a conscious, intentional choice. While realising I was enough was a huge shift for me, it didn't come naturally at first. I started one morning with one small reframe where I said to myself: *'I'm going to try believing I'm already enough. Just for today. Just to see what happens.'*

I still had to catch myself in my thoughts. Reset. Remind myself of this new way of thinking, but over time, something fundamental shifted.

I didn't lose my ambition, I found freedom and lightness in it. The drive was still there (I am still me), but it wasn't desperate any more. I became intentional about what I focused on, letting go of what didn't serve me and that liberated me more than you can imagine.

I didn't achieve less, I just stopped over-functioning. And weirdly, I performed better. My standards didn't lower, I just stopped sacrificing myself to meet them.

My days looked different:

- I moved intentionally with more presence.
- I stopped chasing the next thing to feel complete.
- My to-do list became shorter and more realistic.
- I let go of not answering every email with lightning speed.
- I stopped filling my days with back-to-back meetings and, instead, planned for thinking time.
- I said 'no' without guilt (for the first time in years).
- I took care of myself first and then started my day serving others.

- I let my family see the real me — wobbles and all.
- I didn't wear a blue suit and collapse in a foyer; I wore sequins and showed up rested.

The surprising result?

The world didn't end when I stopped proving. It finally began.

The ongoing practice it became

This wasn't a one-time revelation. As I practised this way of being, it began to reshape my inner narrative. This practice became a life-changing way of being that required daily work and discipline. Some of that practice meant that I:

- forgot the next day and had to remember again
- slipped back into proving and had to catch myself
- battled the old voice (the blue suit voice) that said 'not enough'
- chose the new voice that said 'already enough'.

I was constantly resetting. Tuning into my inner voice. Sitting with my slipped behaviours and reminding myself of my intention. Over time something fundamental had shifted:

- I now knew there was another, more fulfilling way.
- I'd experienced what 'enough' felt like and believed it.
- I couldn't unknow it and began to trust it.
- I couldn't unsee the cost of the blue suit mentality.
- I felt lighter and wanted more of that.

A new practice emerged: Every morning, before I reached for my phone, before I jumped into doing, I would say:

- I have already done enough.
- I already am enough.
- I already have enough.

And then I would ask myself: *What do I want to create from here? If there is one thing I want to do today to create impact — what is it?*

- Not from emptiness, from sufficiency.
- Not from proving, from being.
- Not from scarcity, from abundance.
- Not from perfection, from authenticity.
- Not from busyness, from spaciousness.
- Not from the blue suit, from wholeness.

And so my inner reset began.

😷 Unmask exercise: What if?

Let's take a moment to imagine how it would really feel if you truly felt you had done enough, were enough and had enough. Stop. Close your eyes. Take three deep breaths. Picture your blue suit moment — you know, the time you pushed yourself to collapse trying to prove your enoughness.

Now imagine: What if, before that moment, someone had whispered:

▸ You've already done enough.
▸ You already are enough.
▸ You already have enough.

How would that moment have been different? What would you have done? Would you have let go of the proving to the point of collapse?

The mindset shift: From proving to enough already

Take a moment to reflect on an intentional choice that is within your control right now. You could let your old mindset run, telling you to prove your worth through effort and sacrifice, or you could reframe it and own your power by being enough as you are. Your reframe might look like this:

Old mindset	New mindset
I must do more, be more, sacrifice more to earn my worth.	I have done enough. I am enough. I have enough. I choose from here.

What this mindset shift actually means

You might be reading this and feeling some internal anxiety bubbling up at the thought of being told to slow down or do less or stop. But it's called a mindset *shift* for a reason:

It's not	It is
• Lowering your standards	• Separating worth from output
• Achieving less	• Trusting you're not behind, you're exactly where you need to be
• Becoming complacent	
• Abandoning ambition	• Choosing sustainable excellence over unsustainable sacrifice
• Settling for mediocrity	
• Never pushing yourself again	• Leading from wholeness, not depletion
• Stopping improvement and learning	• Achieving without self-abandonment
• Being excellent all the time	• Pushing with purpose, not proving
	• Being intentional about your actions
	• Showing up as your authentic self

What this meant for me was that this life, this moment, this imperfect beautiful now is enough. That I didn't need more to be happy, I just needed space and capacity to show up for each day. That sufficiency didn't mean stagnation, it meant choosing and creating my best life from abundance not depletion.

What changes:

- You stop sacrificing now for a mythical 'later'.
- You make decisions from wholeness, not scarcity.
- You experience your life instead of managing it.
- You practise radical acceptance (more on that in Mindset shift #2 on page 95).

You reclaim your energy:

- No more exhausting yourself to prove your worth.
- You feel lighter and more capable as you are not weighed down by endurance.
- No more self-sacrifice as proof of commitment.
- Sustainable excellence instead of unsustainable striving and efforting.
- No more blue suit moments or you catch them before they break you.

You deepen your impact:

- You create from contentment/fullness, not emptiness/depletion.
- You lead from presence, not performance.
- You influence through authenticity, not proving or perfecting.
- You have greater impact that you can enjoy as it has not cost you.
- You do your best work from a place of knowing not proving.

You live your life:

- Relationships deepen (you're available, not performing).
- Deep contentment returns (you're experiencing and being, not managing and desperate).

- Freedom and capacity expand (you're choosing, not compelled).
- You show up in all your shapes and forms (in my case, navigating my health), good days and bad days — and it's simply enough.

What I know to be true

✧ You have done enough. You are enough. You have enough. The blue suit? You can take it off now.

✧ That story you've been telling yourself (that you need to prove your worth through endless effort, that rest is something you earn, that 'just enough' equals failure) is a lie, and it's silently breaking you.

✧ You don't need to collapse in a hotel foyer to prove your value. You don't need to sacrifice yourself at the altar of everyone else's expectations. You don't need one more achievement to finally feel worthy.

✧ You weren't born to live like this. You were conditioned to believe that excellence requires suffering. That worth is earned through relentless performance. That slowing down or achieving without it costing you equals failure.

✧ Because excellence doesn't require self-destruction. Success doesn't demand you disappear in the process. And ambition doesn't need to cost you your health, your relationships and your sense of self.

✧ The people who truly matter don't need you to be perfect. They need you to be present. They need the version of you that has energy left over for what actually matters. They need you — not the exhausted, performing, proving version.

✧ The relief you're seeking? The permission you're waiting for? The proof that you've finally done enough? It's not coming from the next achievement. It's not coming from the moment you choose to believe what's already true: You are already enough.

✧ The person beneath the performance? You're still here. And you've been enough all along.

Once I stopped proving my enoughness, I had to face a terrifying question: Who was I without the performance? Without the titles, the roles, the achievements? Who was left?

I'd spent so long being the 'happy warrior', the overachiever, the one who could handle anything, that I'd forgotten who I was underneath it all. I'd lost myself in the labels. And I needed to find my way back.

That's where the next mindset shift begins: reclaiming the woman beneath the performance. Dropping the masks. Discovering who you actually are when you're not busy being who you think you should be.

And the real you is waiting.

😣 Unmask exercise: Enough already check-in

Perhaps you are still not quite convinced yet. That inner voice that keeps you proving and efforting is operating on outdated information. It's time to question its logic, and tame this way of thinking…to truly step into your enoughness.

Name the fear

Complete the following sentence with brutal honesty and write down everything that comes up. Don't edit. Just write the raw fear.

(continued)

'If I stop efforting and proving myself, I'm afraid that...'

▸ people will see I'm not actually that good
▸ I'll lose my place at the table
▸ I won't be enough as I am
▸ I'll become ordinary/invisible/forgotten/lesser
▸ I'll discover I was never really worthy/enough.

That's your inner critic's script. The story it tells to keep you running.

Question the evidence

For each fear, ask: *Is this actually true or is it just a thought? Is this a belief that I need to let go of as it no longer serves me?*

Then answer:

▸ Have I ever stopped efforting before? (A sick day watching trashy TV, not checking your emails, showing up to a meeting and just listening, or a time you said 'no' without saying why.)
▸ What actually happened? (Did people judge you? Make you feel bad? Did you lose respect? Or did nothing catastrophic occur?)
▸ Am I confusing 'what if' with 'what is'? (Is this based on something that happened, or something I'm imagining? Remember not every thought you have is necessarily true or a good one.)

Often, the evidence doesn't support the fear.

Rewrite the script

Your inner critic's old script probably goes something like: *'You must prove your worth through endless effort or you'll fail.'*

What's the new script? The one that's actually true? Examples to inspire you:

Old: If I stop over-delivering, people will see I'm not exceptional.

New: My value comes from who I am, not from exhausting myself.

Old: If I let go of perfectionism, I'll become mediocre.

New: Excellence doesn't require self-destruction.

Old: If I stop sacrificing myself for everyone else, I'll let people down.

New: The people who matter don't need me to put myself last to prove I care/am worthy.

Choose one new script to practise for the next 24 hours using the steps in the next unmask exercise.

😣 Unmask exercise: The 24-hour already enough practice

Now, having unmasked what is really sitting behind your mindset shift, let's begin by practising for just 24 hours to see how it feels to operate this way. Just 24 hours…

The practice: For one full day, operate from this belief: *I have done enough. I am enough. I have enough.*

Think it sounds simple? Try it. Your brain will resist, trust me. That's the point. That's where the insights come. It will be challenging at first. Lean in and simply notice.

(continued)

> *Morning ritual (five minutes):* Before you reach for your phone, before you check email, before you jump into doing, write down three:
>
> ▸ things you've already done that are enough (your version of the blue suit pitch, the achievements you've dismissed)
> ▸ ways you already are enough (without achieving anything)
> ▸ things you already have that are enough (that you've been overlooking and are grateful for).
>
> *Throughout the day:* When you catch yourself in 'blue suit mode' (over-efforting, over-proving, over-pleasing):
>
> ▸ Pause
> ▸ Ask: *Am I doing this from enoughness or from proving?*
> ▸ Choose: *What would I do if I already believed I was enough in this moment right now?*
>
> Notice where you:
>
> ▸ over-deliver (doing more than enough to prove worth)
> ▸ over-explain (justifying your existence)
> ▸ over-function (sacrificing yourself to earn belonging)
> ▸ over-please (say 'yes' when you want to say 'no')
> ▸ over-perfect (make sure everything is perfect)
> ▸ add unnecessary effort (your version of not going home for four days — over-polishing that presentation).
>
> Practise strategic enoughness:
>
> ▸ Do what's needed and no more — not what's needed plus 50 per cent to prove yourself. Scary, I know!
> ▸ Show up as you are, not who you think you should be. Just be in a meeting, not forcing the outcomes.

> ▸ Create boundaries that honour your enoughness: take a
> lunch break, finish on time, say 'no' to a meeting even!
>
> *Evening reflection:*
>
> ▸ Grab your journal and write your thoughts in response to
> these statements:
> ▸ Where did I feel resistance to 'enough'?
> ▸ What happened when I chose to trust my enoughness? Was
> I more present? How did I feel? What was different?
> ▸ What became possible when I stopped proving? How
> present was I in the moment?
> ▸ What would my 'blue suit moment' look like if I believed
> I was already enough?

✨ Glittering truths ✨

If you only remember three things from this chapter, make them these:

1. Your worth isn't earned through sacrifice, it's inherent

The blue suit moments (the all-nighters, the collapsing in hotel foyers, the relentless proving), they weren't badges of honour. They were symptoms of a fundamentally flawed equation: that your value depends on your output. It doesn't. Never did. The exhaustion you feel isn't proof you need better systems, it's proof you're operating from a mindset that was never true: that your enoughness must be earned. You were always enough. The achievement just made it harder to see.

2. The three stories destroying you (I haven't done enough, I'm not enough, I don't have enough) feed each other and create an impossible standard you'll never meet

It's not because you're not working hard enough, it's because the finish line doesn't exist. You're not running towards something, you're running from a fear. No amount of achieving will make that fear go away. The relief you're seeking isn't coming from the next achievement, it's coming from the moment you choose to believe what's already true: You are already enough. Right now. As you are.

3. Enoughness isn't the end of excellence, it's the beginning of sustainable excellence

When you stop proving your worth through endless effort, you don't achieve less, you stop over-functioning. You perform better because you're no longer sacrificing yourself to meet standards. The difference isn't lowering your ambition, it's finding freedom in it. The drive is still there, but it's not desperate any more. It's intentional. That's where real impact lives, not in the frantic chase, but in the conscious choice to create from sufficiency, not scarcity.

6

MINDSET RESET #2: DROP THE MASKS

The world doesn't need another perfect performance—it needs you

> 'All that glitters is not gold.'
>
> —*William Shakespeare*

Too professional

Six months into my new role at Ogilvy in Australia, the CEO called me into his office for my performance review. 'There's only one thing you need to work on', he said before he rushed to his next meeting. 'You're too professional. Just...loosen up a bit. You're too polished.'

His words hit like a challenge I couldn't ignore.

I sat with this feedback wondering how on earth I could unlearn my high-performing professional way of operating. It felt so natural to me to perform this way. So I decided to experiment with being less polished and more...me.

I started small:

- softening my emails with the occasional emoji
- sharing my weekend (even though I'd secretly worked through it)
- swearing occasionally to seem 'less corporate'
- shakily asking my team for support when I needed it
- admitting to clients when we needed more time (despite the sinking feeling of failure)
- laughing when someone told me I had lipstick on my teeth instead of blushing in shame
- trading the heels that killed me for flats.

In short, I let down my polished mask a little and started being me. Oh, it was hard to let go of the polish. To be vulnerable. To be not perfect. To not have the answers. It felt unnatural. If I'm honest, it felt like I might be found out for who I really was and not be seen as successful or having it 'all together'. My hands literally shook the first time I admitted I didn't have an answer in a client meeting.

I wasn't prepared for what happened next.

When I stopped performing perfection and started showing up as human, something magical shifted. My team didn't just respect me, they trusted me.

As I let down my white pearly feathers of perfection (aka the swan), I got a bit 'duck like', sharing that I needed their help or owned my mistakes out loud (shock, horror). I was not prepared for the gift of connection. It made me a better leader — go figure! And more than that, it felt effortless and lighter. I stopped worrying about my performance and showed up as me. I stopped pretending and found that my energy shifted.

I was the imperfect duck not the perfect swan.

But this was just the beginning, because what I didn't know then was that my illness would strip away every mask I'd ever worn and force me to confront who I was underneath all the performance.

Maybe you've been told to 'loosen up', 'be more human' or 'just be yourself'. And maybe, like me, you had no idea how to do that without feeling like you'd lose your edge, your authority, your place at the table. That's because you've been performing so long, the mask feels like your face.

Why I wore masks

I didn't set out to become a shapeshifter. I learned early that being myself wasn't enough.

At work, I was the unflappable leader who never showed struggle. At home, I tried to be the perfect mother while secretly exhausted. In public, I was the successful woman who made it all look effortless. Alone in my car between roles? Lost, depleted, not knowing who I was without the performing.

I remember standing in the queue at Harris Farm with my son one day. Dosed up on steroids. Exhausted from the day, squeezing in the food shop before heading home to cook dinner. My son was impatient, dancing around. I turned to him in a rage I couldn't control (the steroids made me explosive) and snapped, 'Get in the line,' at such velocity my voice reverberated across the store. Everyone stared.

My son turned to the lady behind us and sweetly said, 'Don't worry, it's my mum's rhoids'. I wanted to run from the store so embarrassed for losing it. I had cracked — well, the steroids had cracked me — and my darling son was apologising for me.

I thought these masks were protecting me. Keeping me safe. They were actually erasing the real me. It was hard to keep the masks on as my life fell apart. And they were costing me big.

My mask of pretending I was well when I was not. My mask of being the perfect mum while juggling the demands at work and illness. The pretending I was fine to my loved ones so they didn't worry when all I needed was a hug. The baseline despair underneath 'having it all together' mask was breaking me.

Here's the core belief that keeps overachievers performing: *Being myself isn't enough. I must perform to be successful, respected, valued.*

For overachievers like us, authenticity feels dangerous. Performance feels safer. We learned early: being yourself isn't enough. You got rewarded for performance, not authenticity. Vulnerability looked like weakness. 'Being professional' meant hiding your humanity.

I was rewarded for keeping the masks on. Celebrated for being so strong, resilient and inspiring as I navigated my health crisis while working in a big job. Convincing myself I needed to and didn't want anyone to see the real shame and cluster fuck that was my life. It was beyond exhausting. The fear of being found out. The shame of being me. And now, when in a room with other leaders, I realise I'm not alone. Here's the masks I see most commonly. Different version:

- at work (polished, in control, never vulnerable)
- at home (trying to be present while exhausted)
- with friends (the fun one, the capable one, never the struggling one)
- in public (together, successful, effortless).

Maintaining multiple personas is like running multiple operating systems simultaneously. Eventually, the system crashes.

The stories behind the masks

The more I'm in rooms with leaders sharing vulnerably, the more I notice these common stories we tell ourselves about what it means to be the leader:

- Leadership means sacrificing yourself for others.
- Showing vulnerability makes you weak.
- I can't bring my whole self to work.
- I have to have all the answers.
- I can't afford to make mistakes or admit them to others when I get it wrong.
- If I'm not busy, I'm not being productive or valuable.
- If I'm not in control, everything will fall apart.
- Asking for help makes me incompetent.
- I have to be a certain kind of leader to be successful.
- Everyone else's needs matter more than my own.
- I have to have it together all of the time.
- I need to get everything done on my to-do list.

Sound familiar?

The three overachiever myths

And for me, there are three common overachiever myths that I see time and time again that truly affected how I could lead with impact and not lose myself in the process.

Myth 1: Leadership means martyrdom

I get it. We think we need to sacrifice ourselves at the altar of leadership. Yet research[23] reveals there's a double-edged sword to self-sacrifice where this style of leadership actually backfires.

When you're constantly sacrificing yourself in ways that feel performative rather than genuine, your team actually starts doing less, not more. They stop going the extra mile. Instead of inspiring people to give their best, martyrdom leadership creates teams who show up, do exactly what's required and nothing more. You've traded authentic influence for compliance. And compliance never built anything extraordinary.

Myth 2: Strong leaders hide their struggles

Here's the counterintuitive truth that most overachievers resist: your struggles aren't weaknesses to hide. They're leadership superpowers waiting to be unlocked.

Research shows that psychological safety (created when leaders show vulnerability and authenticity) dramatically increases team performance.[24] When you show up human, acknowledging when you don't have all the answers, you give your team permission to do the same.

The result? You create environments where people take smart risks, share breakthrough ideas and collaborate without fear.

Myth 3: Authority comes from having it all together

One of the biggest lie overachievers tell themselves? That authority comes from never showing uncertainty.

When leaders drop the mask of constant competence, their teams don't lose respect, they gain trust. Authentic authority is built on self-awareness, honest communication and values-driven behaviour that's consistent whether you're in the boardroom or the break room.

Which of these myths do you recognise in yourself? Which one costs you the most energy to maintain? Write it down — this awareness is your starting point.

These three myths create the foundation for the masks we wear. And once you understand why you're performing, you can start to see what you're actually performing: the three specific masks that keep overachievers trapped in the exhausting cycle of shapeshifting.

The overachiever's masks: The psychology of performance

In boardrooms across the globe, I see the same cast of characters: brilliant leaders trapped in performances they can't escape.

These aren't behaviour patterns to identify, they're mindsets that trap you in performance. Deep beliefs about what it takes to be successful, respected, valued. Each mask represents a core belief that you can't show up as yourself and be successful. And each one is costing you everything.

The competence mask: 'I have it all together'

- Nothing throws you (on the surface).
- You never admit uncertainty or not having answers.
- You perform confidence even when drowning in fear.
- Exhausting yourself to ensure you're over-prepared.
- Hair perfect, outfit flawless, never a crack in the facade.

You believe: If you admit you don't know, you'll be exposed as a fraud.
The cost: You're isolated, exhausted from maintaining the facade, and your team is afraid to admit when they don't know either.

The perfection mask: 'I never make mistakes'

- Everything is flawless, polished, one step ahead.
- You over-prepare for everything.
- You're constantly worrying about what's next.
- You hide any sign of struggle or failure.
- You're the first to arrive, last to leave and respond at all hours.

You believe: Mistakes mean you're not good enough.

The cost: You're exhausted, your standards make others afraid they'll fall short, and you're missing the present moment while managing imaginary futures.

The people-pleasing mask: 'I'll be whoever you need'

- You shapeshift for different audiences.
- Always saying 'yes'; nothing is ever a problem.
- You're losing yourself trying to meet everyone's expectations.
- Never wanting to 'rock the boat' with a differing opinion.
- Morphing to match whoever you're with.

You believe: Acceptance is earned through performance.

The cost: You've lost track of who you actually are. You become whoever others need and disappear in the process.

I coached a senior chief marketing officer who'd become a chameleon, shapeshifting to match each leader she worked for. It earned her a reputation for 'managing up' brilliantly but the cost was her team's trust. More than that, she'd lost herself, finding little contentment in achievements because she didn't know who she was without performing.

These masks aren't protecting you — they're erasing you.

The goal isn't to eliminate your capabilities. It's to choose when to use them rather than being enslaved by them. Sometimes you need to be the decisive leader. Sometimes you need to be the caring human or ask for help. The art is knowing which moment calls for what and never losing sight of the person underneath the role.

> ### 🎭Unmask exercise: Your masks
>
> Take a moment now to reflect on these masks:
>
> - Which mask stood out to you?
> - How does this mask serve you? What are the gifts of this mask to you? For example, perhaps you believe that having it all together means that people won't realise what's really going on.
> - What are the costs of this story to you? For example, it's exhausting to pretend I have it together all the time when I could really use some help.
> - How would it feel to let this mask down and let others see the authentic you?

The exhausting art of performance

Here's what no-one tells you about being a high-functioning overachiever: You become a master at performing and making it look effortless while exhausting yourself in the process. Different from traditional collapse, this is about staying productive while feeling utterly depleted. You deliver exceptional work while your insides are screaming. You show up brilliantly while secretly wondering how much longer you can keep this up.

Research shows[25] performing different identities across contexts increases anxiety and depletes energy. Authenticity correlates with wellbeing; inauthenticity correlates with depression.[26]

Carl Jung called this 'the persona': the social mask you wear in social situations, the compromise between who you are and what society expects. He distinguished between two parts of us:

1. *Your persona:* The social mask: your titles, roles, professional identity. Beautiful performance but exhausting to maintain.
2. *Your authentic self:* Your integrated personality including all your human bits: natural, authentic, sustainable, effective, real.

Jung believed[7] the goal wasn't to eliminate your professional capabilities but to consciously choose when to use them rather than being trapped by them.

The persona becomes dangerous when you over-identify with it and are unable to differentiate between your role and who you are. So if you lose your job, it can feel like you have lost your sense of self and you can't separate who you are from what you do.

The 'true self' vs 'false self' split creates internal fragmentation. Integration (being the same person across contexts) reduces stress. When you show up as the same person at work and at home, you're less depleted. Like my chief marketing officer client, you lose track of who you actually are. You become whoever others need, and disappear in the process. And no-one wants that!

For me, I wore different masks everywhere:

- *At work:* the unflappable leader who never showed struggle
- *At home:* trying to be the perfect mother while falling apart inside
- *In public:* the successful woman who made it all look effortless
- *Alone in my car between roles:* exhausted, lost, not knowing who I was without the performing.

I thought these masks were protecting me and allowing me to achieve as they covered up my not-so-perfect self. They were actually erasing me.

When the mask becomes the person

Here's the brutal truth about performing: eventually, you forget who you are underneath the performance. You become so good at being what others need that you lose track of what you actually want and sometimes who you really are.

And the costs aren't just personal, they're professional too:

- Your impossibly high standards make your team afraid they'll fall short.
- Your people wait for you to solve problems rather than thinking for themselves.
- You have decision-making fatigue from constantly making the 'right' decisions under pressure.
- Your over-professional swanning results in team disengagement where people don't really know you or connect with you.
- When in crisis, you put up walls and pretend you're 'fine' when it's obvious you're not, which makes others feel they can't support you.

The first five years of being sick, I was in complete denial. I truly believed I could cure this incurable disease through sheer effort. After all, I'd fixed everything else in my life that way.

After losing everything that I had defined as success, I did what every overachiever does when they hit rock bottom: I set a new, more impossible goal. I would become the best high-performing sick person. I would rise from the tsunami that nearly killed me and prove that no matter what life threw at me, I had what it took to achieve. Because if I wasn't achieving, who even was I? Slowing down felt more dangerous than dying.

Here's what I didn't understand or want to admit: I didn't know what to do with myself other than perform. Without the running, chasing, deadlines, firefighting, I was completely lost.

I was completely unable to process having no meetings other than the hospital treatments, spacious amounts of time to rest, and no money to shop or do the things I would dream of when I was achieving and had no time. Nope, I was unwell, everything was an effort, no goals other than to stay alive and yet I told myself I needed to keep performing to keep the roof over our heads which was a reality for me, yet I didn't think to let my mask down too much as I was so ashamed of falling sick. I didn't want anyone to know my inner pain of having to fight for my life, so I put on another mask.

I decided to be a high-performing sick person. No challenge too small for me, right? Because here's what no-one tells you about overachievers — we don't just fear failure, we fear being seen for who we are, our authentic imperfect self. So I just put on another mask and kept going...

😣 Unmask exercise: Your mirror

Take a moment to step back from the busy and let down your mask a little. It's just us. Draw a line down the middle of a page. On the left-hand side, list all of the performance masks you wear at work, at home, with friends, on LinkedIn, Instagram, with your family of origin; for example, 'I am the super organised mother'. Then, on the right-hand side, for each persona, write what's the truth — what do you really feel, what are you struggling with, what are you really wanting and who you actually are when you are not performing.

The performance masks	The truth: The authentic me
The super organised mother	*Always rushing and panicking that I have missed a school notice or event…* *Comparing myself to the other mothers who seem more organised than me*

Look at the gap between the two columns. The gap is the cost of the masks. The distance between your performance and you showing up as your authentic self.

Reflect honestly:

- How much energy am I spending maintaining all of these personas?
- What would change if I showed up as myself instead?
- Who would I be if I stopped performing all these personas?
- What aspects of myself do I hide or fear others finding out about?

Why I had to stop performing leadership

I had to realise and acknowledge that I was a fabulous performer. You will remember my *Hello, Dolly!* tap dancing ways from Chapter 3, it was my default way to lead as a performer. To put on a good show. I even had a presentation tone of voice I had to let go of. I was not aware I was doing it most days as it had become my default.

So, to try a new way of leading was brave and scary for me so I had to understand the science before I was convinced I could let go of this learned way of leading and actually let people in to see the real authentic me.

Here's what makes authentic leadership neurologically superior to performed leadership:

- *Trust builds faster:* Studies using brain imaging show that when people interact with authentic leaders, their brains release oxytocin, the bonding hormone that creates psychological safety.[27] This isn't just feel-good chemistry, it's the biological basis of high-performing teams. I experienced this when I let my team know about my health journey rather than pretending I was 'fine'.

- *Decisions improve:* Authentic leaders access more of their prefrontal cortex capacity because they're not burning cognitive resources on impression management.[25]

- *Stress decreases:* When you align your leadership with your authentic self, you experience less chronic stress.[28] Lower stress means better immune function, improved sleep and sustained high performance without the crash.

- *Innovation increases:* Teams with psychological safety (created by authentic leadership) generate significantly more innovative solutions[29,30] because people feel safe sharing unconventional ideas without fear of judgement.

The bottom line for overachievers: Authentic leadership isn't about becoming more vulnerable, it's about becoming more impactful. It's not about working less, it's about working with neurological and psychological principles that multiply your impact while reducing your effort.

When my masks became unsustainable

There were three life-changing moments that stripped away my masks and brought me back to being my authentic self.

Moment 1: What do you do?

The first time I ventured out socially while on sick leave, I dressed up, trading my pyjamas for a gorgeous pant suit. I covered my pale, sick face with makeup, really making an effort to present well. I was exhausted from treatment yet mentally bored out of my tree. I was excited for this school event as a departure from my hospital regime.

I remember one of the more polished working mums — a lawyer, I think — coming up to me with that confident smile I recognised from my old life.

'So, what do you do?' she asked brightly.

Blank. Complete blank.

The awkward pause stretched between us like a chasm. 'Oh, I'm just taking a break from work at the moment', I finally managed, not wanting to be the downer at this event with my illness.

Her expression shifted. 'Oh, have you lost your job?'

The question hit like a slap. Me? Lost my job? That would never happen to someone like me. 'No, I'm just taking time off to focus on my family', I responded quickly.

She looked at me for another beat, decided I wasn't worth talking to, and simply walked away. No goodbye. She just…left.

I stood there alone, processing what had just happened.

Why did I need to lie? Why couldn't I share my reality? Was the shame so deep? Was I not worthy of conversation if I didn't have a job title to offer?

My empathy for mums who choose not to work went deep in that moment. So this is how it feels to be judged by achievement. As if I had nothing to offer without my professional credentials.

It was a brutal wake-up call about how much I measured my own worth by my salary, my title, the external markers I had defined as success. That hierarchy of introduction I'd perfected: the job first, the person second. When I was achieving, it had meaning. Now? I no longer fit into my old category of 'working overachiever mum doing the juggle'. Now I was 'just' the sick mum with few prospects.

A small voice inside my head whispered, 'If I'm not achieving, what's left?'

I realised my definition of success wasn't even mine — and neither was my identity. I had been introducing myself wrong my entire life, leading with what I did instead of who I was.

Later, at another hospital appointment: Occupation: __________.

I stared at the blank line on the admission form, pen hovering. For the first time in my adult life, I had no idea what to write.

Six months ago, I would have filled this out without hesitation. *Senior Executive. Leader. Marketing.* Those words used to roll off my tongue like a prayer I knew by heart.

Now? Nothing.

The nurse looked at me expectantly. 'Having trouble with that one?'

'You could say that', I managed, finally scrawling 'N/A' in the box.

But, really, I was having trouble with everything. Without my title, my status, my endless meetings, who was I? Yes, mother, wife, daughter, friend… but who was I without the roles I performed?

I was lost. And it was the beginning of something real — finding my way back to me.

I had to accept that my entire identity was fused to what I did. I'd attached labels to my life: the boss lady, the capable one, the together mum, the high-performing sick person. My illness stripped all the personas. The roles I performed — professional, mother, wife, friend — each with different masks, had to change as I could no longer maintain them. I only had enough energy left to just be me.

Performance had become impossible. Standing there without any of the personas — just me, myself, and I — I was terrified: 'If I'm not the capable one, the strong one, the together one — who am I?'

Psychologists call this 'identity fusion', when you become so merged with your role that you can't separate who you are from what you do. As overachievers, we're particularly vulnerable to this because we take such value in our titles as part of our success story.

As I mentioned in chapter 5, I had two options: desperately cling to labels that no longer fit, or step into the terrifying unknown of just being me. Fleur. Without the titles, without the achievements, without the armour of professional success.

The question was: Would she be enough?

When did what you do become who you are? When did your job title become more important than your name? You might not be able to answer that, perhaps because it happened so gradually you didn't notice. But standing here now, ask yourself: If I stripped away the titles, the roles, the achievements, would I know who I am?

Moment 2: Red lipstick as revolution

I remember the first time I decided to re-enter the normal world — not for treatment, not for necessity, but just to be among people again. I stood in front of my bathroom mirror like an athlete preparing for a comeback after an injury.

My reflection showed a stranger. Steroid-puffy face, thinned hair, clothes that no longer fit the body I once knew. The woman staring back at me looked nothing like the executive who used to command boardrooms.

But her eyes? Her eyes were different. Clearer. More honest.

I reached for my red lipstick, the same shade I'd worn to every important meeting, every presentation where I needed to feel powerful. Only this time, I wasn't trying to convince anyone of my competence. I was announcing my existence.

The type of chemo I had didn't necessarily result in hair loss, but hair thinning. I was also on high-dose steroids, so I'd gained about 30 kilos. Apart from a greenish pallor, my illness was invisible, which was both good and bad.

People often didn't take my illness seriously. They thought I was being dramatic. And since 'sarcoidosis' isn't well understood, it felt like people thought I wasn't really that sick.

I didn't want to identify as a sick person. I wanted to be *seen*, but on my terms.

Red lipstick became my war paint.

This wasn't about denial or performance. This was about reclaiming visibility on my terms. Each time I applied that red lipstick, I was making a statement: despite how I looked, despite what I was going through, I was still here. Still choosing. Still me. Bright red lippy and all!

Over the years to come, I used clothes as my way of expressing myself. Holding on to the real me underneath my battle scars. I traded my superwoman cape for sequins. Like my decision to dress up for chemo, I let my wardrobe help define my identity and intentionally shape how I showed up to the world.

I decided that life was for celebrating. Why not wear sequins? Why not use the fancy china, burn the nice candles and live for today? I stopped being superwoman trying to play all these roles that I thought I 'should' and let go of the expectations I had placed on myself to be everything to everyone.

I decided to retire my superwoman cape for good, and everything changed.

The cape had been heavy, woven from expectations, responsibilities and the crushing need to be everything to everyone. When I finally retired it, I discovered something surprising: The lighter I became, the more real I felt.

Sequins became my new friend. They catch the light without trying too hard. They're joyful without being serious. They announce: 'I choose to sparkle, even in the dark'. An act of defiance. No matter what life throws at me, I'm shining bright despite it all.

What's your version of red lipstick or sequins? The thing that reminds you who you are underneath the roles, the masks, the performance? The choice that announces: I'm still here, still choosing, still me.

Moment 3: The meeting where I stayed silent

Six months back at work, part-time. I could only manage three days a week, but I was trying to do a week's work in three days. Old habits die hard.

The pressure was on for a huge brand campaign. The team was stuck on a problem. There was tension between them as we needed to crack it fast as the client presentation was the next day when I wouldn't be in the office to support them. The urge to fix it, solve it, take it on was rising within me. I wanted to rescue. That's what I always did. That's what made me valuable. That's what proved I was still the capable one despite being sick.

My team looked at me, waiting for me to help. They knew I'd jump in. I always did. Internally, I was at war with myself knowing that if I gave them a solution, I would need to help them see it through. If I didn't, they may lose valuable time. But I knew I had to step out for treatment the next day, and truthfully, I was exhausted. My body was already at its limit from just showing up.

So I did something I'd never done before: I stayed silent. The team waited for me to jump in. I just sat there. The silence stretched. My team shifted uncomfortably. Finally, I spoke: 'I know you're all completely capable of solving this one. I can't wait to see where you get to.

Please feel free to bounce the options with me when you're ready before the end of today as I will be out from tomorrow.'

And then I left the meeting.

No efforting. No proving. Just being the leader without performing the hero.

They solved it. Without me. And they were proud of themselves.

I'd been so busy performing 'the one with all the answers' that I'd been robbing them of the chance to lead. My mask wasn't protecting them, it was limiting them.

And me? I had energy left at the end of the day. For the first time in months. I could face my next treatment not depleted but ready knowing that my team had it covered.

The mask I'd worn (I must solve everything to prove I'm valuable) wasn't just exhausting me, it was preventing real leadership. When I dropped it, something unexpected happened: my team stepped up. And I got myself back.

Where are you performing when presence would serve better? Where are you solving when silence would empower? The mask of 'I must have all the answers' isn't just exhausting you, it's limiting them. What would happen if you stayed silent? If you trusted your team enough to step back?

The mindset shift I had to make

Somewhere between losing my labels, choosing the red lipstick and showing up as authentically me, I stopped asking:

'Who should I be right now?'

And started asking:

'Who am I when I'm not performing?'

This mindset shift wasn't about becoming someone new, it was about stopping the performance and revealing who was already there.

What I had to accept:

- I didn't know who I was without the performance.
- I'd built my entire identity on roles that weren't me.
- I'd been shapeshifting so long, I'd lost track of myself.
- The masks weren't protecting me, they were erasing me.

What I had to let go of:

- performing competence when I was struggling
- being 'the strong one' who never needed help
- shapeshifting for different audiences
- managing others' comfort with my reality
- the belief that being myself wasn't enough.

Without the masks, I discovered someone who:

- was scared but showing up anyway
- needed help and could finally ask
- was imperfect and discovering that was okay
- was enough without the performance
- didn't have to take herself so seriously all the time
- felt lighter and connected more deeply with others.

It wasn't comfortable, but it was real.

So what does it really mean to be authentically you? It is not about finding yourself in the 'Byron Bay vibes' way. It is not about becoming someone else. It's simply about stopping the shapeshifting of trying to be someone else and being consistently you. You will know it when you do it as it feels different. It comes from a place of knowing, not criticism or judging yourself. It's being brave enough to tune into what matters to you, how you want to be each day and then practising vulnerable moments to let your mask down to see how it feels. It's about being wholeheartedly you...

Authenticity is:

- being the same person across all contexts (work, home, public, private)
- showing up honestly about where you are (not performing where you think you should be)
- letting people see your struggle (not just your success)
- claiming your preferences, boundaries, voice (not morphing to please).

Once I let go of who I wanted to be and simply be me, I chose to be intentional about what I did and didn't do. I had limited energy being in a chronically ill body, I had less time than most as I was only able to work part-time, and I was determined to not repeat the same learned behaviours of taking on too much and ending up in a heap. I got better at understanding where I added value. What I did that no-one else could do. What my team really needed from me. What my clients needed from me.

I tuned into my body constantly as my energy waxed and waned depending on my treatment cycle. I was performing in a way that felt not at the cost of me, that was true to my limits. It allowed my team to take accountability and for me to be the leader they needed. I owned my capability limits by asking for help or suggesting that I did not own a deliverable alone given my unpredictable body. I found freedom in just being me, with intention focused on what I could do, not what I couldn't. It was a daily check-in practice where I constantly managed my own expectations of myself and then communicated with others what I could do.

The biggest, unexpected thing that happened was that when I stopped performing, connection with others deepened. I no longer felt alone.

- My children got me back (not the perfect mum version) and could be themselves more.
- My relationships became real (not transactional based on performance).
- My work became authentic and energising (leading from truth, not perfection).
- I got myself back (finally present in my own life).

The masks had promised safety. Authenticity delivered a better way of being.

The moment I stopped performing who I thought I should be, I found the only power I'd ever actually needed: permission to be myself.

What belief about masks are you ready to question? That performance equals safety? That authenticity equals weakness? That you can't be successful and yourself? That's the mindset shift waiting for you. And on the other side? The real you — who's been enough all along.

The mindset shift: From performing to being you

Part of shifting your mindset is catching the unhelpful thoughts as they happen. You might catch yourself in this reframe:

Old mindset	New mindset
I must be perfect/pleasing to be accepted. If people see the real me, they'll realise I'm not enough.	I am enough exactly as I am. The world doesn't need another performance, it needs the messy, brilliant truth of who I actually am.

What this shift actually means

Making this shift requires courage: dropping the mask to be your vulnerable, authentic self. But it's not what you think. Here's what it actually means — and what it doesn't:

Dropping the masks is not	Dropping the masks is
• Oversharing • Having no boundaries • Being unprofessional or careless • Not recognising what is appropriate for which environment • Using authenticity as an excuse for poor behaviour • Letting yourself go or lowering standards	• Being the same person across all contexts (integration, not fragmentation) • Showing up honestly about where you are (not performing where you think you should be) • Letting people see your humanity (struggle alongside success) • Understanding what is appropriate and how to navigate yourself in different contexts • Claiming your voice, preferences, boundaries (not morphing to please) • Leading/parenting/relating from truth, not performance

What changes

When you begin to practise dropping your mask and showing up as yourself, you will begin to notice a real shift from within:

You stop exhausting yourself:

- No more maintaining multiple personas
- No more shapeshifting for different audiences
- No more performing confidence while drowning inside

You reclaim your energy:

- Authenticity requires less energy than performance
- Being one person is simpler than being many
- Integration is easier than fragmentation

You deepen connection:

- People connect with truth, not performance
- Vulnerability creates intimacy
- Your relationships become real, not transactional

You find your voice:

- You stop asking 'What should I say?' and start saying what's true
- You stop morphing to please and start claiming your boundaries
- You lead from authenticity, not from perfection

You come home to yourself:

- You're finally present in your own life
- You know who you are (because you're not performing who you should be)
- You're enough exactly as you are.

What I know to be true

✧ The people who matter don't need your perfection. They need your presence. Your team doesn't need the 'unflappable leader', they need a human they can trust who has their back. Your colleagues don't need the 'always has it together' version, they need someone real enough to learn from and honest enough to speak their mind. The people you're trying to inspire? They're watching the mask go on, and not connecting with the person underneath.

✧ When you drop the performance, you don't lose respect, you reclaim yourself and find real connection. Better yet,

(continued)

you stop exhausting yourself being who you think you should be at work and who you think you should be at home and start leading as who you actually are.

✧ Being yourself everywhere takes less energy than performing for everyone and losing yourself in the process. You don't have to shapeshift any more. You don't have to remember which mask to wear in which room. You can just…be. And this was a game changer for me as I navigated my illness.

✧ Authenticity is braver than any performance. It takes more courage to show up as yourself than it does to maintain the polished facade. But that courage is where real leadership lives. Where trust is built. Where influence actually happens.

✧ You don't have to choose between being successful and being yourself. The most powerful leaders are the ones who've learned to integrate both professional excellence without personal depletion. Your worth isn't tied to your performance. And your leadership can be both ambitious and authentic.

Here's what changes when you drop the masks:

✧ Your team stops waiting for you to solve everything. They start thinking for themselves and share their mistakes early rather than hide them. Your colleagues start trusting you with their struggles because you've shown them yours. Your influence deepens because people follow humans, not performances.

✧ And you? You finally get yourself back. The energy you've been pouring into maintaining the facade becomes available for actual leading. For actual living. For showing up as the leader you actually are, not the one you think you should be.

So here's your choice: Keep performing and lose yourself in the process or drop the masks and discover that the unmasked version of you is far more powerful than any persona you've perfected.

The question isn't whether you're strong enough to keep performing. You've already proven that.

The question is whether you're brave enough to stop.

✧ You've released the proving (Shift 1: Enough already).
✧ You've dropped the masks (Shift 2: Authentic self).

Now you're ready for the final inner shift: releasing the grip on control and accepting what is (Shift 3: Loosen your grip).

😣 Unmask exercise: The RAIN practice

When I finally stopped performing long enough to ask who I was without the roles, I realised I didn't actually know. And maybe you feel that too. If you weren't constantly 'delivering' or 'holding it all together', who would you be?

This is where Tara Brach's RAIN practice[31] became a lifeline for me. It's simple, practical...no incense or chanting required. It helps you catch yourself in that split second when you feel the urge to perform: when someone questions your work, when you walk into a high-stakes meeting, when you sense you've let yourself or someone down. That moment when your brain screams 'prove yourself' and you reach for the mask. RAIN creates a pause between the trigger and your automatic response, giving you space to choose authenticity over performance. This practice will help you regulate, gain perspective and ease the feelings so you can stay true to yourself instead of defaulting to who you think you need to be.

(continued)

> ▸ *Recognise* what's happening. Notice the identity you've been clinging to (e.g. the achiever, the strong one, the one who never drops the ball).
>
> ▸ *Allow* it. Instead of fighting your thoughts and feelings or shoving them down, let yourself feel the weight of them. Notice any one dominant thought or feeling. Yes, it might feel uncomfy sitting with this. That's part of the honesty.
>
> ▸ *Investigate with kindness.* Check in with your body. Where are you carrying this thought or emotion? The tight jaw? The knot in your stomach? How would you describe it? A heavy rock, a sharp piece of glass, a butterfly knot in your tummy. Listen and notice without judgement.
>
> ▸ *Non-identification.* Release. Let go of those thoughts or feelings that are making you want to wear your mask to keep you safe. These feelings or thoughts are just that—you can choose to let them shape you or simply let go of them so you can continue to show up as your authentic self.
>
> Pause here. Take a breath. Try this for just a few minutes. Notice what comes up when you stop identifying only with what you *do*. Imagine if you stopped *doing* or *delivering* and just did you. No outcomes. Because the truth is, your worth has never been tied to your output even if the world taught you otherwise.

😔 Unmask exercise: The 7-day 'show up as you' practice

Here's the problem: you can't change a pattern you're not aware of. Right now, you're performing on autopilot—switching between masks so seamlessly you don't even realise you're doing it. We're not practising self-awareness for the sake of self-awareness, this is strategic intelligence gathering so you can make the real mindset shift happen and show up as you.

For the next seven days, you're going to track exactly when, where and why you perform. Think of this as data collection on your highest-cost behaviour. Because here's what I've seen with every overachiever I work with: The energy you spend managing masks, code-switching between contexts and being different versions of yourself in different rooms is the same energy you could be using to actually lead, create impact and enjoy your life.

This exercise will show you where you default to performing instead of being mask-free and doing you. Noticing what triggers send you straight into autopilot. And by day seven, you'll have a better sense of what it costs you to keep performing, and what it feels like when you don't.

Seven days. Five minutes, twice a day just noticing and being intentional about how you show up. That's the investment. The ROI? You'll finally see your patterns clearly enough to change them.

For seven days, be the same person in every context.

Morning intention: 'Today, I will be me, not a performed version of me in every interaction.'

Throughout the day: Try these micro practices.

- Before meetings: Ask 'Am I showing up as myself or my role?'
- In conversations: Share one genuine insight, struggle, uncertainty or bravely say 'I don't know', even when it feels vulnerable.
- Making decisions: Ask 'What would my authentic self choose here?'

(continued)

> ‣ When shapeshifting starts: Pause. Notice the mask
> appearing. Choose authenticity instead.
>
> **Evening reflection** (two minutes):
>
> ‣ Where did I show up authentically today?
> ‣ Where did I catch myself performing? What triggered it?
> ‣ What felt different when I was just being me?
>
> *By day seven:* Notice what happens when you stop performing.
> You're more present. Connection deepens. And you finally come
> home to yourself.

✧ Glittering truths ✧

If you only remember three things from this chapter, make them these:

1. The masks aren't protecting you, they're costing you

The competence mask never admits uncertainty. The perfection mask hides mistakes. The people-pleasing mask morphs to match whoever you're with. You built them to feel safe, to be successful, to be accepted. But here's the truth: the more you perform, the less of you remains. The more energy performing takes and less connection you build. The polished 'have it all together' professional who never shows struggle or failure? That's not leadership, that's pretending and isolating. The shapeshifter who becomes whomever the room needs? That's not adaptability, that's self-abandonment. The costs are real and happen every day without you even noticing.

2. Authenticity isn't weakness, it's neurologically superior leadership

When you show up as yourself, trust builds faster (oxytocin in the brain), decisions improve (23 per cent better strategic thinking), stress decreases (lower cortisol), and innovation increases (32 per cent more breakthrough ideas). This isn't about becoming more vulnerable for vulnerability's sake. It's about understanding that authentic leadership multiplies your impact while reducing your effort. The people you're trying to inspire? They're not connecting with the mask, they're waiting to trust the human underneath. Your team doesn't need the 'unflappable leader', they need someone real enough to learn from.

3. The real you — imperfect, honest, messy — is more powerful than any persona you've perfected

Without the titles, the roles, the performance, you were always whole. The person who admits they don't have all the answers builds more trust than the one who pretends they do. The leader who shows up human gives permission for others to do the same. Stripped of labels, you don't lose value, you reclaim yourself. The question isn't whether you're strong enough to keep performing. You've already proven that. The question is whether you're brave enough to stop. Because authenticity is braver than any performance. And the unmasked version of you? You've been enough all along.

7

MINDSET RESET #3: LOOSEN YOUR GRIP

Your power lives in what you choose, not what you control

> 'Between stimulus and response there is a space. In that space is our power to choose our response. In our response lies our growth and our freedom.'
>
> — *Viktor E. Frankl*

This is as good as it gets

I walked into my immunologist's office thinking I'd finally turned a corner.

Seventeen rounds of chemo behind me. Months of clean eating, daily green juices, meditation, yoga and resting — I'd taken radical responsibility for my healing. I'd controlled every variable I could: diet, stress, sleep, supplements. If modern medicine couldn't cure my sarcoidosis, I'd find another way through integrated medicine and self-compassion.

Sarcoidosis is a rare autoimmune disease with no known cause and no known cure. It causes inflammatory cells to attack your organs. For me, it was in my lymph nodes, which meant it could show up anywhere in my body. Most people respond to treatment. I didn't. I'd already endured 17 rounds of chemotherapy (more than three times what most cancer patients receive) and years of immunotherapy infusions, countless steroids and treatments. My body was annihilated by the very treatments meant to save it.

But I felt better. My energy was returning, I had a few headaches, but I attributed that to the detox. Surely all my efforts were paying off.

My immunologist (the best in Australia) looked up from my file. 'Fleur, I've reviewed your latest scans.'

I leaned forward, ready to hear good news.

'The sarcoidosis has spread to your brain.'

The room tilted.

'As you know there is no cure for sarcoidosis. Your liver is not coping with the treatment load. We've exhausted all standard protocols. You've failed every treatment available to keep the disease under control.'

He paused, choosing his words carefully.

'This is as good as it gets for you. We need to prepare for the possibility that things may not improve from here.'

I sat there, numb.

Despite everything

Despite the clean diet, the radical self-care, the sheer force of will. Despite rounds of chemo. Despite years of immunotherapy infusions. Despite being treated by the best immunologist in the country. Despite controlling every single variable I possibly could. I was worse, and there was nothing left to try.

Every strategy I'd used — clean eating, positive thinking, willpower, self-compassion, biohacking — had changed nothing. My body was failing. The treatments had failed. And I might die.

I'd built my entire life on the belief that control equals safety. If I just worked hard enough, tried hard enough, I could force outcomes. I could fix anything. I could achieve my way out of any problem.

My body shattered that delusion in one appointment. No amount of green juice was going to save me. No guru, no protocol, no amount of effort. I'd already done more than most people could survive, and it wasn't enough.

The real transformation I needed wasn't external, it was internal. And it started with something I'd spent my entire life avoiding: accepting I was in a sick body I could not control.

Not managing it better. Not trying harder. Not finding the miracle cure. Or fixing myself.

Just… accepting: It is what it is. I cannot control whether I live or die. I cannot control how much time I have. I cannot control my body's response to treatment.

And the question that emerged: 'If I can't control whether I live, can I accept that reality and still choose how I show up while I'm here?' What I can choose is how I respond to my reality and how I want to show up for life despite it being out of my control.

Learning to live — fully, bravely, honestly — when you can't control what happens next, that's where the third mindset shift really happened for me. Loosening the grip on control, leaning into accepting my reality and living my best life, despite it all.

Maybe your body hasn't betrayed you like mine did, but something has: a redundancy you didn't see coming, a relationship that ended despite your best efforts, a project that failed no matter how hard you worked. That moment when control was ripped from your hands and you realised the truth: some things cannot be fixed, managed, or achieved your way out of. That's where this shift begins.

Holding the grip tightly

I'd built my entire life on a single idea: control equals safety.

If I just worked hard enough, I could force outcomes. I could fix anything. I could achieve my way out of any problem.

Somewhere along the way, control became my competitive advantage. It's how I succeeded. It's how I stayed ahead. It's how I proved I was capable. And it felt like competence but, in reality, it was anxiety in action.

As overachievers, we operate with three types of control.

1. Outcomes control: If I work hard enough, I can guarantee success

- You believe effort always equals results.
- You're devastated when things don't work out despite doing everything 'right'.
- You can't rest until you know how things will turn out.
- If something fails, it's because you didn't control enough variables.

2. People control: If I manage everyone's emotions, everything will be okay

- You over-explain to control how others perceive you.
- You take responsibility for feelings that aren't yours to carry.
- You smooth over conflict before it even happens.
- You believe if you can just anticipate everyone's needs, nothing will go wrong.

3. Future control: If I prepare for every scenario, nothing can hurt me

- You live constant 'what if' scenarios.
- You can't be present because you're managing tomorrow.

- You have back-up plans for your back-up plans.
- The more you anticipate, the safer you'll be.

Research shows[32] that people with perfectionist and achievement-oriented traits have lower tolerance for uncertainty. Your brain experiences 'not knowing' as significantly more threatening than the average person's, which is why you feel compelled to control, plan and manage everything obsessively.

But here's what you need to know: You can't actually control any of it. That redundancy you didn't see coming. That question you didn't have the answer for. That moment when things didn't go as you had planned. That annoying cough that won't go away.

You're exhausting yourself trying to control the uncontrollable: other people's reactions, external circumstances, outcomes that depend on factors beyond you.

You're living in isolation. When you're controlling everything, no-one can actually help you because you won't let them.

You're missing your life. While you're managing every outcome, you're not experiencing any of it.

And your body is keeping score whether or not you acknowledge it. Chronic tension. Constant headaches. Disrupted sleep. Digestive issues. Brain fog. Baseline exhaustion that rest doesn't fix. Your body is paying the price for a control system that was never meant to run 24/7.

As my body became my greatest teacher, I realised some things cannot be fixed, controlled or achieved your way out of. That's where real change begins. It comes from:

- fighting my reality to radical acceptance
- 'I need to fix this' to 'it is what it is' and 'I choose how I show up'
- control to presence and surrender.

Control isn't keeping you safe, it's keeping you stuck. The harder you grip, the less control you actually have (aka my disease had spread to my brain despite it all!).

Power pause: Which type of control exhausts you most?

Here's the uncomfortable truth: somewhere along the way, like me, you became convinced that if you could just control enough variables, you'd finally be safe. Successful. Worthy.

So let me ask you this: Where are you exhausting yourself trying to manage the unmanageable right now?

- **Outcomes:** Are you trying to guarantee outcomes, desperately needing every presentation, every project, every single thing to land perfectly?
- **People:** Are you managing everyone else's emotions, smoothing over tensions, anticipating reactions before they happen to keep everyone happy?
- **Future:** Are you preparing for every possible scenario or catastrophising about the future, running scenario after scenario in your mind, preparing for disasters that haven't happened and probably never will?

Notice which one made your heart race as you read it. That instinctive gut panic. That's your nervous system recognising where you're exhausting yourself trying to control the uncontrollable. That's the grip you need to loosen.

> ### 🎭 Unmask exercise: The grip test
>
> Write down everything you're currently trying to control: other people's responses, your boss, your body's response to stress, whether you get the promotion, how quickly the project moves, what your team does, what people think of you, the perfect presentation... Look at your list.
>
> *Circle what's actually in your power:* Ask 'Which of these can I actually control?' Not influence. Not hope for. Not work really hard at. Control.
>
> Circle the ones that are genuinely in your power. (Hint: It's probably only your own choices and responses.) Cross out everything else.
>
> *Then do this:* Rip that page in half. Burn it. Bin it. Physically release it.
>
> This is a visceral act of surrender. It's your body learning what your mind knows: You can't control most of what you're trying to hold on to.
>
> Reflect:
>
> - How much energy were you spending trying to control what you can't?
> - What would change if you accepted reality instead of fighting it?
> - What space opens up when you stop trying to control it?

The shift I had to make

Before I got sick, I had perfected the art of control.

I micromanaged every detail because I believed outcomes depended entirely on my effort. I managed everyone's emotions, smoothing over potential conflict before it could even surface.

Every scenario was mapped, every variable was accounted for. I thought I was being strategic. Thorough. On top of things.

Turns out, I was just running a very sophisticated anxiety management system, and calling it 'leadership'.

My illness became my toughest teacher — the kind that doesn't let you skip class or negotiate extensions. When life hands you something you literally cannot fix, manage or achieve your way out of, you're left with one question:

Can you accept what is and choose your response from there?

I learned (slowly, painfully, reluctantly) to let go of controlling what was never mine to control: my body's response to treatment, whether I'd live or die, how much time I had left.

That created space to focus on what I actually could control: the next breath, the next hour, how I showed up in this moment.

And here's what I didn't see coming: When I loosened my grip enough to let others help, everything got lighter. Not easier... lighter. Less exhausting. More possible. And I was no longer alone.

That's where the real shift began.

It is what it is (and it's still beautiful)

The second control mindset shift came when I realised that I was exhausting myself fighting my reality.

When struggle hits, whether it's a devastating diagnosis, career setback or even a shitty day, our instinct is to fight reality. We rage, we bargain, we wear ourselves thin battling circumstances completely outside our control.

Here's what I learned the hard way: The more we fight what is, the more it wears us down. All that energy spent resisting reality is energy stolen from actually dealing with it.

This is where overachievers like us get stuck. We're professional problem-solvers, right? We fix things. We make the impossible happen. We don't accept — we overcome.

But acceptance isn't giving up. It's getting strategically smart about where you invest your limited energy. When you accept what you genuinely can't control, you become powerful at influencing what you actually can.

There's a concept in *te ao* Māori (the Māori worldview) that helped me understand this: *kia kaha*. It's often translated as 'be strong' or 'have courage', but it's so much deeper than that. It's the inner strength that comes from accepting what is, not forcing what isn't. It's about bending with the storm, not breaking against it.

At school, I remember being told about the mighty *tōtara* tree. During fierce storms, while other trees would break fighting the wind, the *tōtara* would bend and flow, its roots deep and strong. The storm would pass, and the *tōtara* would stand tall, not because it fought the wind, but because it knew when to yield.

I used to think *kia kaha* meant never showing weakness, never surrendering — being courageous and resilient always. But watching my body fail despite my best efforts taught me that sometimes having courage means surrender, not battle. Sometimes the strongest thing you can do is accept what you cannot change and choose your response from there.

For me, understanding that true *kia kaha* sometimes meant surrender, not battle, changed everything.

The power of five simple words

Saying to myself 'It is what it is' became my lifeline.

It wasn't giving up, it was accepting what was so I could focus on what I could actually influence. To not react to things outside of my control, but respond to them. It was the only thing I could control.

- When I got my diagnosis: *It is what it is.*
- When treatment made me gain 30 kg: *It is what it is.*
- When I lost my career identity: *It is what it is.*
- When my disease spread to my brain: *It is what it is.*

I remember lying in bed after a brutal treatment, feeling sorry for myself and angry at the unfairness. My daughter asked if I could do colouring in with her. My first instinct was 'no': I was too sick, too busy fighting my reality. Then I stopped. *It is what it is.* I'm sick, yes, but right now, my daughter wants to snuggle up and colour in. That's what's actually happening.

We coloured in for hours. It became one of my favourite days of that entire year.

When my immunologist told me the disease had spread to my brain, when they said 'prepare for the worst', when my body refused to obey any command I gave it, I had a choice: keep fighting reality and exhaust myself further, or radically accept what was true and choose my response.

Radical acceptance became my way of surviving, my way of regaining control by focusing on what I could rather than fighting what I couldn't.

The blue esky revelation

The best part about my children's private school wasn't the facilities, it was the community of parents. One mum, Lorene, approached me during my treatment and asked how she could support us. I batted away her generous offer, saying we had it all under control. The belief underneath my resistance: 'I should be able to handle this. If I accept help, I'm failing.'

She persisted. 'I really want to help. Perhaps I can do a food roster?' A little voice inside whispered *yes please.* 'How wonderful,' I managed. 'Just to get us through the next few rounds of treatment.'

I knew I had to accept that my body had limits I could no longer deny. Control had to die so I could survive, and I knew I needed to accept my limits and not do this alone.

Lorene put an esky bin outside my front door so as not to disturb my recovery. Next minute, a roster was in full swing. Each day, post-treatment, I'd find prepared meals, magazines, flowers, little cards, chocolates inside that blue esky.

It wasn't just the meals, it was kindness from people I'd never met, who were generously helping our family in our time of crisis. Some days I wept opening that box. One parent didn't have time to make something so had 'guiltily' gone to a nearby restaurant and bought us dinner, apologising for not having the time to cook.

That was the first crack where I realised that accepting my limits wasn't giving up. It was the first honest assessment of reality I'd made in years. And that honesty created space for help to arrive.

Here's what finally surrendering and asking for help taught me: People actually *want* to help. I'd felt like I needed to do it all alone. This support went on for nearly 12 months. I will never be able to thank everyone who kept me going during the darkest time.

As leaders, we're taught that asking for help signals weakness. That not knowing the answer somehow disqualifies us from the role. I carried this belief into my sickest moments, convinced that admitting I needed support would somehow diminish my authority or burden others unnecessarily.

When I finally stopped fighting what I couldn't change, something extraordinary happened: The energy I'd been burning in resistance became available for actual living. The mental space I'd been using to argue with reality freed up for real solutions. The tight grip I'd been holding on to outcomes I couldn't control? I loosened it, and found I could finally breathe.

I wasn't giving up, I was getting strategic. Focusing my limited energy on what I could actually influence: my response, my choices, my presence.

The science behind surrender

When we stop fighting reality, our nervous system can shift out of constant fight-or-flight mode. Research on self-compassion[33] shows that accepting ourselves and our circumstances (rather than fighting what is) reduces stress and creates psychological space for healing and problem solving.

What radical acceptance is	What radical acceptance is not
Seeing reality exactly as it is (not as you wish it were)	Giving up or becoming passive
Stopping the exhausting fight against what you cannot change	Avoiding action where you can make a difference
Understanding and honouring your limits (body, capacity, control)	Accepting unacceptable behaviour from others
Giving control less power over your peace	Pretending you're fine when you're not
Creating space between what happens to you and what you do about it	'Everything happens for a reason' toxic positivity
The foundation for real change	Lowering standards or not trying

What I had to radically accept

It was not easy, but I realised that I needed to sit with my reality and finally accept:

- my body was sick, and I couldn't fix it
- treatment might not work and I might die
- I couldn't guarantee I'd see my kids grow up
- I needed help I couldn't give myself

- I had limits I couldn't push through any more
- I had to let go of the life I had dreamed of to live the one I was in
- I couldn't be the perfect mum but rather the imperfect real present one
- we may never get to own a home again
- we had lost everything I had worked so hard for, and what mattered was not what we had but the time we had together.

It wasn't that I wanted to accept these things, but fighting reality was costing me the life I had left.

> **Power pause: Naming it to tame it**
>
> What's the one thing you need to radically accept that you keep fighting? Your body's limits? That your capacity has limits? Someone else's reaction? That outcome you can't force? Say it out loud right now: 'It is what it is'. Notice what happens in your body. Resistance? Relief? Both? That's the beginning of the shift.

What happens when you loosen the grip

Once I accepted reality, I had to release the grip on trying to change what I couldn't.

I let go of:

- trying to force my body to heal through willpower
- managing everyone's emotions about my illness
- planning a future I couldn't guarantee
- controlling outcomes I had zero power over
- the belief that if I just tried harder, I could fix this.

This wasn't giving up. It was giving control less power over my inner peace. The less I tried to control, the less control controlled me.

I also had to face limits I'd spent my life denying, including that my:

- body had limits (I couldn't push through pain any more)
- capacity had limits (I couldn't do everything alone)
- control had limits (I couldn't force outcomes no matter how hard I tried).

Overachievers hear 'limits' as 'failure', but limits are just reality. And reality was the only place I could actually operate from. When I stopped fighting what was and started accepting what is, something unexpected happened. Space opened up. Space to:

- breathe without constant hypervigilance
- ask for help without shame (because I'd accepted my limits)
- be present without managing imaginary and scary futures
- choose my response to what was actually happening (not what I wished was happening)
- live in uncertainty without terror consuming every moment.

Acceptance didn't make everything okay, but it made facing my impermanence possible. The moment I stopped trying to control my illness, I found the only power I'd ever actually had: my response to reality, not my ability to change it.

Here's what asking for help actually taught me about leadership: The strongest leaders aren't those who never need support, they're the ones who know how to mobilise it strategically.

What asking for help actually does

Here's what I believed about asking for help: I thought it would make me look like a failure, like I couldn't solve it all on my own. But when my body forced me to finally let people in, I discovered gifts I was completely unprepared for — that asking for help:

- gives others purpose and connection
- builds genuine influence — people follow leaders they trust, and trust requires letting others see your humanity
- creates deeper relationships than surface-level interactions
- models healthy boundaries
- creates psychological safety giving others permission to admit when they are struggling too
- shows that high achievement doesn't require self-destruction
- multiplies your capacity without depleting others' — one person carrying everything creates bottlenecks; distributed support creates flow.

Brené Brown's research on vulnerability is well known. Her research shows that asking for help activates what she calls 'empathy loops': when we allow others to support us, it strengthens social bonds and increases collective resilience. The shame we feel about needing help? That's actually our nervous system's outdated survival mechanism trying to keep us safe by keeping us isolated.

The greatest leadership shift isn't learning to have all the answers, it's learning to ask the right questions and knowing who to ask. Asking for help isn't admitting weakness, it's demonstrating the emotional intelligence to leverage collective wisdom.

Every time I said 'I've got this' when I clearly didn't, I robbed someone of the chance to contribute. I robbed myself of support and felt alone in moments when I needed help. And I robbed my team of seeing what healthy leadership actually looks like, and allowing the space for them to rise up to the challenge.

Ask yourself: What if the strength you think you're showing by never asking for help is actually limiting everyone's chance to step up and shine? What help are you refusing right now because you think you 'should' be able to handle it alone? What would it cost you to ask? What's it costing you not to? The blue esky bin taught me that people want to help, but they can't if you won't let them.

Katie's story: When the plan falls apart

Katie had been intentionally shaping her career since she was 14 years old. Every job, every move, every milestone was all carefully orchestrated. Success meant career achievement and financial security. The safety that came from always knowing what was next.

Her pathway was crystal clear. She never questioned it. Planning and preparing — that was her safety net. That was how she controlled outcomes.

And it worked brilliantly.

When she moved countries (not once, but multiple times) she always had a job lined up before she arrived. By 30, she had it all. The achievement checklist perfectly ticked off. Married. Two children. A house. The career trajectory she'd mapped out when she was four was unfolding exactly as she'd envisioned.

Until her job was pulled while she was on maternity leave.

She realised something fundamental: She couldn't control what happened to her, and more dangerous still, her entire identity was 100 per cent linked to her job. When that was taken away, she felt like she'd lost herself.

But Katie did what Katie always did: She adapted. She rebuilt. She got back in control. And for years, it worked brilliantly (again).

Then, finally, she achieved something even harder: balance.

She'd navigated her way into the perfect role, one that allowed her to be present as a mum, maintain financial security, show up for her children without crushing guilt. She wasn't growing professionally, but everything else was in place.

For the first time in her adult life, Katie wasn't striving. She was living.

She'd even said to her husband while they were on holiday just weeks before, lying by the pool watching the kids play: 'This all feels too good to be true.'

He'd laughed. 'You've earned it. Enjoy it.'

Two days later, everything shattered.

Two days before her 41st birthday, Katie received a calendar notification: 'Notification of proposed changes.'

Her stomach dropped. Having already made almost 40 people redundant herself just seven months earlier, she knew exactly what those words meant. It was corporate code for 'your job is ending'.

Deep shock hit. *How did this happen? I was careful. I was strategic. And still blindsided.*

Everyone around her kept saying she'd be okay. She was capable. She'd land on her feet.

Platitudes. Well-meaning reassurances. But no-one stopped to let her feel how she actually felt. She had no space for acceptance. No permission to sit with the reality that her entire identity had just been stripped away again.

Everyone expected resilience, but Katie didn't feel resilient. She felt terrified.

The kids' needs didn't stop. Private school fees were coming, looming like a noose around her neck. The mortgage didn't pause. The household bills kept coming. The life she'd built required the income she no longer had.

She started saying 'no' to invitations for events, lunches, catch-ups. Contract work kept the lights on, but it wasn't security. The woman who always had a job before she moved countries was now scrambling for short-term work to pay the bills.

Every day was a battle between control and surrender. Between the person she'd always been — the planner, the achiever — and the person life was forcing her to become: someone who had to trust without guarantees.

Months passed like this and still nothing was in her control.

Then came the moment everything shifted.

Katie was in church one Sunday morning. Broken. Exhausted from fighting reality. The congregation was singing:

> *Jesus, I was tossed in the water, but I never went under*

> *No, You were always on time.*

> *And Jesus, when I went through the fire, You were right there beside me*

> *No, You were always on time.*

Tears were streaming down Katie's face. Always on time.

Not on Katie's time. Not according to her carefully orchestrated plan. On God's time. The universe's time. The timing she couldn't control no matter how hard she tried.

And in that moment, something inside her finally released.

She'd been fighting so hard to make her next opportunity happen now. To force the timing. To regain control.

But she couldn't. And the harder she tried, the more exhausted she became.

She finally understood: Her next thing would not be on Katie's time. It would happen when it was meant to happen. She needed to let go. Not give up — let go.

She started trusting that whatever she focused her time and energy on now would serve what came next — without needing to know what or when. She leaned into the uncertainty instead of battling it. And she felt an overwhelming sense of peace and freedom from fear. Not because circumstances changed, but because she stopped demanding they change on her timeline.

An inner knowing settled in. She could control how she showed up. She could control the relationships she built. She could control her willingness to stay open to possibilities she hadn't orchestrated.

What she couldn't control (and what was destroying her by trying) was when and how it would all come together.

What Katie knows now

Katie's still figuring out what comes next, but she's doing it from a foundation she'd never built before: trust in timing she can't control. Katie reflects:

> The moment that unexpected sucker punch lands, fear is real because we lose our grip on controlling the outcome. We are confronted with the terrifying truth: We cannot control the uncontrollable external forces that shape our lives.

> But in the depth of that pain, and, in my case, faith becomes a powerful call to let go of control. Instead of desperately fighting to regain that external control, our work must pivot inward. We stop focusing our energy on what was lost or can't control and find the courage to explore and trust what's next.

> We counter our fears by digging deep into places we didn't know existed before and choosing to take on life with a lion's spirit to survive. Because it is only in that space of uncomfortable growth that courage becomes a state of mind, where we lean into a continued willingness to fail and true possibility can be found.

Katie's story isn't about failure, it's about the illusion of control shattering and discovering that the freedom on the other side of that shattering is more powerful than the grip ever was.

What are you gripping so tightly that it's exhausting you? What reality are you fighting that acceptance might free you from? What would change if you trusted the timing you can't control and focused your energy on choosing your response instead?

You don't have to wait for a crisis to make that choice. The relief you're seeking? The freedom you're craving? The peace you've been chasing through achievement and control?

It's on the other side of surrender.

The mindset shift: From control to acceptance

You cannot control most of what happens in your life, but you can control how you respond — and that's where your real power lives. Here's the shift that changes everything:

Old mindset	New mindset
I must control outcomes, people's reactions and future scenarios to be safe. If I let go, everything will fall apart.	I cannot control most of what happens, but I can control my response and accept it is what it is.

What this mindset shift actually means

Before you dismiss this as giving up or settling, here's what acceptance actually means:

Acceptance is not	Acceptance is
• Giving up on what matters to you • Lowering your standards • Abandoning your ambition • Losing control • Becoming complacent • Chaos or loss of structure • Pretending everything is fine • Letting the world happen to you • Weakness	• Achieving without exhausting yourself • Giving yourself permission to stop fighting what already is so you can focus your energy on what matters • Separating what you can control (your response) from what you can't • Trusting the process even when you don't know where it is heading • Leading from presence and alignment, making choices that serve both your impact and wellbeing • Liberating yourself from constant anticipation and scenario planning • Being intentional about your response • Showing up for what is, not fighting what isn't • Having the courage to trust yourself, others and life — even when things don't go to plan.

What this meant for me was that this life, this moment, this imperfect beautiful now is enough. I don't need more control to be safe, I just need space and capacity to show up for each day. Loosening my grip didn't mean giving up, it meant choosing and creating my best life from acceptance not resistance.

What changes:

- You stop sacrificing now in trying to control tomorrow.
- You make decisions from presence, not fear of what might happen.
- You experience your life instead of managing imaginary futures.
- You practise radical acceptance: it is what it is.

You reclaim your energy:

- No more exhausting yourself trying to control the uncontrollable.
- You feel lighter and more capable as you're not gripping so tightly.
- No more managing everyone's emotions as proof you're in control.
- Sustainable leadership instead of unsustainable control.
- No more back-up plans for your back-up plans, or you catch yourself before you spiral.

You deepen your impact:

- You create from acceptance, not resistance.
- You lead from presence, not constant anticipation.
- Influence comes through authenticity, not managing perceptions.
- You create greater impact you can enjoy as it hasn't cost you.
- You do your best work from trust not fear.

You live your life:

- Relationships deepen (you're present, not managing).
- Deep contentment returns (you're experiencing what is, not fighting what isn't).

- Freedom and capacity expand (you're choosing your response, not trying to control everything).
- You show up in all your shapes and forms (in my case navigating my health), good days and bad days and it's simply enough.

What I learned

I couldn't control my illness, but I could accept it, and that acceptance created space to actually live. Not just survive, but be present for the moments that mattered.

I couldn't do it alone but I could honour my limits, and that honesty let help arrive when I needed it most. That blue esky taught me that asking for help makes you human, not weak.

I couldn't guarantee outcomes, but I could show up anyway, and that presence was braver than any illusion of control.

When you loosen your grip on what you can't control, you finally have energy for what you can: your response, your presence, your choice.

The more you can embrace the mindset of 'it is what it is' and choose how you show up within that reality, the better it will be. Not just for your work. For your life. For the people who need the real you, not the exhausted version trying to control everything.

Congratulations — you've done the inner work.

You've released the proving (Mindset shift 1: Enough already).

You've dropped the masks (Mindset shift 2: Drop the masks).

You've surrendered the illusion of control (Mindset shift 3: Loosen your grip).

Now you're ready for The Lived Reset blueprint: the practical framework for how to actually lead and live from this foundation of enoughness, authenticity and acceptance.

What I know to be true

- ✧ Control isn't keeping you safe, it's exhausting you. And you already know it. That's why you're reading this.
- ✧ The grip you're holding—trying to guarantee outcomes, manage everyone's reactions, prepare for every scenario with back-up plans for your back-up plans—is costing you the only thing you can actually influence: How you show up right now.
- ✧ Here's the choice in front of you: Keep gripping tighter, hoping that if you just control enough variables, nothing will go wrong. Or accept that life will happen anyway, and discover that your power doesn't come from controlling outcomes. It comes from choosing your response.
- ✧ The relief you're seeking? The peace you've been chasing through perfect planning? It's not coming from more control. It's waiting in the surrender. It comes from accepting what is. From honouring your limits. From letting go of outcomes you were never meant to carry. From choosing your response instead of trying to orchestrate every variable. That's where freedom lives.

😣 Unmask exercise: The daily 'it is what it is' practice

For the next seven days, practise radical acceptance to anything that happens that is outside of your control. Notice what comes up for you as you experience this loosening grip and face acceptance.

Step 1: Name what you're fighting

Write down one thing you're currently resisting, trying to change or refusing to accept that is beyond your control.

Examples:

- someone's opinion of you — giving you feedback
- your body's response to stress/worry/pleasing/perfection
- a relationship that's ended or not going well
- an outcome you can't guarantee
- your capacity limits as you're asked to take on more
- your children falling sick on a week you need to be at work
- not knowing what to expect in a meeting or an unpredictable response in a meeting
- someone calling out a mistake you've made or a differing point of view.

Step 2: Say it out loud — 'It is what it is'

Don't add qualifiers. Don't say 'but…' Don't plan how to change it. Just: 'It is what it is.'

Notice what comes up:

- grief (letting go of the reality or the outcome you wanted)
- relief (your body recognising truth)

(continued)

> ▸ anger (resistance to limits or other people's points of view)
>
> ▸ anxiety (fear of not controlling what is happening).
>
> All of it is valid. Let it be there.
>
> ### Step 3: Release the grip
>
> Say out loud: 'I cannot control this, and fighting that truth exhausts me more than accepting it.' Physically unclench (fists, jaw, shoulders). Release the grip.
>
> ### Step 4: Find the space and know your limits
>
> Take three deep breaths. Ground yourself in the moment. Lean into what is. Notice what space opens up when you stop fighting what is. See what happens in the moment when you let go and ask yourself 'What's actually possible here given reality?'
>
> ### Step 5: Choose your response
>
> Ask yourself: 'How do I want to show up in this moment?' Not 'how do I control this or change this', but 'how do I respond to what is?' Choose one small action today that honours reality instead of trying to control it.

You've done the hardest work: the inner reset. You've shifted how you see yourself, your worth and your relationship with control. Now comes the practical question: How do I actually live and lead from this foundation? That's what Part III is for — the blueprint for sustainable success that includes you.

✨ Glittering truths ✨

If you only remember three things from this chapter, make them these:

1. Life will happen to you, and your growth comes from the messy parts

No matter how tightly you grip, how perfectly you plan, how many variables you manage—life happens. Moments of suffering. Moments when control is ripped from your hands. Moments when everything falls apart despite you doing everything right. This is what makes us human. And here's the truth overachievers resist most: change is the only real constant. Certainty is an illusion. Your meaning and growth don't come from the outcomes you orchestrated, they come from the uncontrollable, messy moments you couldn't prevent. I found my courage not in healing my body, but in accepting I couldn't. The three types of control—outcomes, people, future—they're not protecting you, they're exhausting you while life happens anyway. Control isn't keeping you safe, it's keeping you from the growth that lives in real life.

2. 'It is what it is' creates the space where real choice becomes possible

Acceptance isn't giving up. It's *kia kaha*: true courage that sometimes means surrender, not battle. Like the mighty tōtara tree that bends with fierce storms instead of breaking against them, acceptance is about strategically choosing where you invest your limited energy. When you stop resisting reality, something shifts: space opens up. Space to breathe without constant hypervigilance. Space to be present instead of managing imaginary futures. Space to choose your response to what is, not fight what isn't. 'It is what it is' isn't resignation, it's the most honest, powerful assessment you can make. And from that acceptance, real possibility lives. The freedom to live the life you have, not the one you're desperately trying to control. That's where the beauty is.

3. Loosening your grip doesn't diminish you, it frees you

The energy you've been burning trying to control everything becomes available for actually living. Relationships deepen when you're present, not managing. Connection happens when you let people see your struggle, not just your success. Your capacity expands when you honour your limits and let others help. The blue esky taught me that loosening the grip frees you to stop performing superhuman and start being human. You stop sacrificing now for imaginary control of tomorrow. You get yourself back. Not the exhausted, gripping, controlling version, the present, responsive, alive version. That's the gift waiting on the other side of surrender.

PART III

THE LIVED RESET

'It is never too late to be what you might have been.'
— *George Eliot*

The map that I wish I'd had

The life you were building (the one that exhausted you) isn't the only one available.

Welcome to The Lived Reset. The blueprint for sustainable success I wish someone had handed me 15 years ago — one that would have saved me from choosing between my ambition and my life.

I created The Lived Reset while rebuilding my life. In hospital beds and boardrooms. Through treatment cycles and strategy meetings. In moments of complete collapse and breakthrough clarity.

You've walked through The Overachiever's Cycle. You've done the inner reset work, the mindset shifts that change everything.

Now comes the part where you make it real.

This is where you build a life where achieving doesn't cost you everything. Where your ambition and sense of self stop fighting each other. Where contentment isn't a fantasy, you'll get to 'one day', it's how you actually live.

This isn't about scaling back your ambition. It's about scaling up your capacity to achieve what matters sustainably, with you in it.

Three pillars. Three non-negotiables. The blueprint I've lived, tested and refined for creating success that includes you.

Let's build your better way.

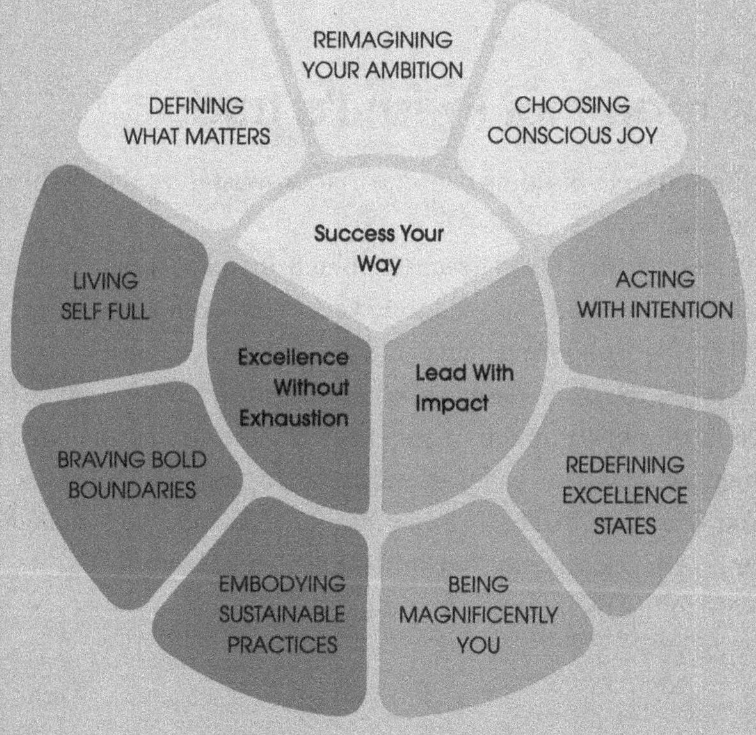

The Lived Reset rests on three core pillars.

Pillar one: Success your way—The why (Chapter 8)

You need to define what success actually means to you—beyond validation and expectations. Reimagine a definition that includes you by defining what matters, reimagining your ambition and choosing conscious joy.

Pillar two: Lead with impact—The how (Chapter 9)

How you lead matters more than how much you do. So next, you need to create real impact consistently by acting with intention, redefining excellence states and being magnificently you.

Pillar three: Excellence without exhaustion—The what (Chapter 10)

Build an operating system that delivers consistently without depleting you. You will do this by defining practices that keep you living self-full, holding brave boundaries and embodying sustainable practices.

Together, these pillars create a foundation for whatever life throws at you—the brilliant moments and the messy ones. They let you navigate your ambition without losing yourself.

Work on one pillar at a time. As an overachiever, you'll want to smash through everything at once. Don't. Be disciplined enough to go slowly. Give yourself space to do the real work.

I've spent the last six years helping thousands of overachievers build their lived reset. Here's what they share: small, intentional shifts that compound over time.

This isn't about perfection. It's about identifying where you're operating from high cost instead of high impact, and making intentional changes that protect your sustainable excellence.

Your reset will be uniquely yours. Your boundaries shaped by your circumstances. Your conscious joy reflecting your personality and values. The leaders who've done this work discovered a better way, and they couldn't go back.

You've got this. You've always had this.

Let's begin.

<u>8</u>

PILLAR ONE: SUCCESS YOUR WAY

From proving to purpose. Reimaging success so it includes you. Legacy beyond the ladder

'What you think you become. What you feel you attract. What you imagine you create.'

—*Buddha*

One question changed everything

It was a Sunday afternoon at the end of a walk. I was alone on the beach, watching the sunset paint the sky. It was one of those moments that should be peaceful.

And I broke.

Not because of one thing. But because of everything.

Years of navigating chronic illness. Years of holding my life together while my body fell apart. Years of working on my mindset, maintaining hope, choosing grace, never giving up. Years of showing up for the people I loved while preparing to leave them.

I'd done everything right. The mindset work. The acceptance. The daily practice of choosing to live while preparing to die.

And I still wasn't living the life I actually wanted. Time was running out.

I'd done the work of being ready to go. I'd accepted that I would. But deep down (in that place I couldn't always admit to), I was desperate to see my kids grow up.

And sitting there on that beach, watching the sun sink into the ocean, I realised something that shattered me: what really mattered to me was crystal clear. And I'd lost so much of those precious moments that gave my life meaning — all the school holidays where I had not taken time off, the bedtime stories I had missed, the fun times with loved ones as I stayed late at the office chasing the next achievement. My daughter's face when I said 'not now, darling' for the hundredth time. The date nights that I cancelled. The version of myself who used to laugh easily, who found joy in small things, who wasn't constantly exhausted or not present to life.

I thought about the years before I got sick. The relentless achieving. The endless proving. The life I'd built that looked so impressive from the outside.

My definition of success had been so flawed it had cost me my life.

It wasn't just the years the disease was stealing, but the years before that when I was healthy and strong and had all the time in the world, and I'd spent it chasing a definition of achieving that cost me my health and didn't make me happy.

And now, sitting here watching that sunset, I could see it so clearly. What mattered. What didn't. What I'd sacrificed for things that never mattered at all.

I am a Māori woman. My culture allows me to understand impermanence in a unique way. We know that death is part of life, that our *tūpuna* (ancestors) walk beside us, that we're part of something larger than ourselves.

But that cultural wisdom didn't erase the grief of what I'd lost or the desperate desire to reclaim what remained.

Here's what hit me in that moment: I was still here. Still alive. Still had time, however much or little that might be.

All this mindset work — all this strength, all this grace, all this refusal to give up — what was I using it for? To survive? To endure? To maintain hope while waiting to die? Or could I use it to actually live? Better than that — live fully?

I wanted to enjoy my life more now as I had nothing left to lose, and, more than that, how could I make my life matter, so others didn't end up here? What if I stopped accepting my death and started reclaiming my life? Not the life I'd been living. Not the definition of success that had cost me everything that mattered. But a life built around what I actually valued. What I truly wanted. What made me feel alive.

I needed to redefine success fast while I still could. So I did what any desperate person does when they finally see the truth.

I begged.

> Universe, God, my *tūpuna*, whoever's listening. Just keep me
> here a little bit longer. Let me see my babies grow up just a
> little bit more. Please.

And if you keep me here, I promise I won't waste it. I promise I'll figure out what really matters. I promise I'll live a life that's actually mine. And I promise I'll help others figure this out before they end up where I am.

And then, sitting there with tears streaming down my face and the sun disappearing into the ocean, I asked the question that would change everything:

If this is it, what do I truly want my life to be?

That question became my daily practice. My lifeline. My way forward.

But answering it? That was a different story entirely.

Defining what matters most

I sat down with my journal the next morning and tried to answer that question: *If this is it, what do I truly want my life to be?* I had nothing. Nothing.

For six months, I drew blanks.

Here I was, a woman who'd built her career on strategic planning and prided myself on goal-setting. Someone who'd navigated impossible challenges and made tough calls. Someone who'd just had the most clarity I'd ever experienced about what really mattered.

Someone who'd done years of mindset work, who knew how to reframe, how to find meaning, how to choose hope in impossible circumstances and keep showing up.

And I couldn't answer the most basic question about what I actually wanted from my life.

The problem? I'd inherited my definition of success from family expectations, societal pressures, comparison with others and that relentless voice whispering 'you're not enough yet'. I realised my definition of success was flawed.

As overachievers, we are world class at setting goals and ambitions. *But here's the thing:* inherited ambition always leads to hollow victories. You might achieve everything you set out to accomplish and still feel empty because it was never authentically yours to begin with.

I'd read Bronnie Ware's *The Top Five Regrets of the Dying*. I knew the number one regret people had at the end of their lives: 'I wish I'd had the courage to live a life true to myself, not the life others expected of me.'

And sitting there with my blank page, I realised that's exactly what I'd been doing my entire life. Living a life of expectations. Other people's definitions of success. Other people's measures of worth. Other people's ideas of what my life should look like, what a 'good' career was, what a 'successful' woman achieved, what 'valuable' looked like.

I'd been so busy achieving brilliantly according to every external marker, I'd never stopped to ask what I actually wanted. I'd spent 40 years building a life that had cost me.

To answer what I wanted, I first had to understand what mattered most to me. Not to anyone else. To me.

So I walked in the early mornings, when my brain wasn't quite awake, so I didn't overthink it. In those quiet 3 am moments, I sat with the question: If this is it, what do I want my life to be?

It started with being values-aligned in the way I showed up for life. Research shows[34] that values-aligned leaders have teams that significantly outperform those led by leaders who make fear-based decisions. When you lead from your core values instead of external pressure, something remarkable happens — your team stops second-guessing every decision and starts executing with confidence.

When you know what you stand for, you don't waste mental energy on analysis paralysis. Your values become your decision-making filter for how you live and lead your life.

This wasn't about impressive values or the ones I thought I should have. This was about my true north: what drove me, what depleted me, what I wanted to be remembered for. This was it. I needed to make it count.

I listened to the clues closely as I showed up for life in the coming weeks. The moments I stumbled. The moments I felt contentment. I noticed what lit me up from the inside, what made me feel satisfied, what drained me. What I yearned deeply for. What I wanted to be remembered for. What people might say at my funeral.

It took six months of staring at that blank page. Six months of sitting with the discomfort of not knowing. Six months of unravelling everything I thought success was supposed to be. But slowly (painfully, honestly) the answers started coming.

So what I really wanted was to:

- *work*, because I love what I do: so many people had told me to 'just rest', but I didn't want to. I loved working.
- *live fully and do what I love*: tuning into what lit me up and letting go of what dragged me down.
- *take care of myself properly* and honour my body's strength: to expend less effort so I had space for genuine self-care.
- *have enough energy* left to laugh, love and play: to actually enjoy the ride.
- *own all that I am*: including my slightly eccentric, over-enthusiastic, sequin-loving self.
- *find a way that wasn't 'all on' then 'all off'*: to balance my extremes without losing my passion (and not at the cost of me).
- *stop living a life of expectation*: to wake up to what really mattered and let go of the hustle.
- *leave a lasting legacy*: to be remembered for my time here, to help others not end up like me.
- *feel enough exactly as I am*: to do me wholeheartedly and enjoy each day.
- *create space for conscious joy daily*: wear the sequins, celebrate the little things, feel alive in my body again.

These weren't impressive goals. They weren't even particularly original, but they were mine. And for the first time in my life, that was enough.

But here's where it got complicated.

The permission slip

Knowing what I wanted was one thing. Actually pursuing it while living in a failing body was another. I had to accept I was trapped in this sick body for the rest of my life, and somehow live my best life within that reality. I found myself holding two truths simultaneously:

- *The tear:* the deep sadness of knowing my impermanence was real.
- *The twinkle:* the realisation that I could still enjoy every day I could put my feet on the ground and move.

But here's what surprised everyone, including me: My ambition and drive remained powerfully strong despite it all. It still pushed me, spoke to me when I was out of options. A little voice inside whispered, *Let's make it count.*

I needed to find the right balance so I could make this life matter, yet I felt I was running out of time, not knowing when I would fall sick again and lose my momentum. I didn't want to operate from fear of time running out but rather from a place of knowing and fullness within.

This tension (the twinkle and the tear) became my teacher.

Then I realised that I needed to give myself permission to live my life. To honour my wants. Like a school permission slip, I was the only one who could make this happen. These weren't LinkedIn-worthy goals, they were my declarative statements for how I wanted to live that honoured what mattered most to me. If this was it, how did I want my life to be?

Here's what I eventually wrote on my permission slip (and, yes, sharing this still makes me feel vulnerable).

If this is it, I truly want to:

- *feel alive in my body again*, not like I'm dragging through my days in a body I no longer recognise
- *be fully present* to my children, their friends, their days, their worries, their dreams
- *feel loved, seen and heard* by my husband Pete: to share my life, my worries, my fears, my imperfections and be loved all the same
- *live by the sea* because it makes me feel happy, calm and soothes my soul
- *wear sequins every day* and dress up for life, especially when I have no occasion
- *hang with my besties more*: be fun-loving, travel together, laugh at each other, hold each other through life's bumps, love each other as we are
- *have conversations that matter*: ones that make me think, learn, challenge and feel like I'm growing
- *create something beautiful* that serves no purpose other than joy
- *feel proud of who I am*, not just what I've accomplished
- *help others not end up like me* and know there is a better way.

I share this vulnerable list, not because it should be your blueprint (it shouldn't), I share it because your blank page is waiting, and it deserves the same radical honesty I eventually gave mine.

The things that will fill your page might be completely different from mine. They might surprise you. They might feel too small or too big or too weird. That's exactly right.

Because here's what I learned staring at that blank page for six months: The goal isn't to create an impressive list that would look good on Instagram or a list of things to tick off. The goal is to reconnect with the part of you that knows what being alive actually feels like: the part that existed before you learned you had to earn your worth through achievement.

Your moment of reckoning doesn't have to wait for a medical diagnosis or a complete life collapse. The central tension you identified earlier in Part II — that inner disconnect between your external success and internal reality — is your invitation to choose differently right now.

Getting clear on what I wanted was one thing. Actually doing it was another.

So I made decisions — real, tangible, life-altering decisions — to honour what mattered while I still could:

- *I moved our family to the sea*. Because it soothed my soul and 'later' wasn't guaranteed.

- *I changed careers* from agency leader to people and culture leader where I could help other leaders grow and take care of themselves along the way.

- *I restructured my work*. Fewer days. More space to rest and figure out my purpose while I still had time.

- *I set brave boundaries* around my energy and time that would have terrified the old me, and I gave myself permission to let go of the small stuff.

- *I started saying 'no'* to what drained me and 'yes' to what lit me up, even when it felt selfish, even when others didn't understand.

- *I stopped treatment*. I was living in a body I no longer recognised. I needed to be in my own body again, for whatever time I had left.

- *I explored my legacy*. What lasting impact did I want to leave? What would give my remaining time meaning?

- *I became present to everyday life* and the simple pleasures I'd been too busy to notice.

- *I had the conversations* no parent wants to have. I shared my hopes and wishes with my children, just in case I wouldn't see them grow up.

- *I let go of friendships* that took more than they gave. I kept the handful of real ones and invested my limited energy there.
- *And I wore sequins.* Burned the nice candles. Did the things that brought me conscious joy. Not later. Now.

This wasn't a bucket list. This was choosing to live the life I had left, not the one I'd been performing.

The question isn't whether change is needed. Deep down, you already know it is. The question is whether you'll choose to take action for yourself in this moment, or continue the cycle until life makes the choice for you.

Reset challenge #1: If this is it?

You don't need to be dying to ask this question. You don't need to fail all treatment. You don't need to sit alone on a beach watching the sun set while preparing to leave your children. But if you're honest, you're probably doing what I was doing: working hard on surviving but not actually living the life you want.

Maybe you're crushing it at work. Maybe you've built impressive resilience and figured out how to navigate challenges with grace. But are you actually living the life you want? Or are you using all your strength just to keep going, to survive, to maintain, to prove you can handle it?

Because here's the uncomfortable truth: Most of us have built impressive lives according to external measures. We've achieved what we were supposed to achieve. Checked the boxes we were supposed to check.

And we've lost what actually matters in the process.

Not to disease. Not to tragedy. Just to a definition of success that was never ours to begin with. You have the opportunity to get that clarity without facing yours.

Most of us are living Bronnie Ware's number one regret in real-time. We're building lives based on what we should want. We're chasing definitions of success that were handed to us. We're proving ourselves worthy according to standards we never chose.

Power pause: Defining success

Let's redefine success together—not after crisis forces you, but while you still have time to live the answer.

Grab your journal and complete this statement: *'If this is it, I truly want my life to be…'*

Then write. Just see what comes up. Don't think. Just write for ten minutes.

Do this every day for a week and notice what matters to you, what bubbles up from deep within. Look at your life through this impermanence lens and question: How different would your life be if this was indeed it? If there are no guarantees from here on out?

If your response is 'no real changes needed'—bravo. If it's a big gulp and an 'okay, now what?' moment, pay attention. None of us know when this is it, yet many of us live like we're invincible until we're not. This is it now: your life, your career. You get to choose how you show up for it.

And if you're sitting there thinking 'I can't just stop achieving. I have responsibilities, people depending on me, bills to pay', don't worry, I'm not suggesting you abandon everything tomorrow. I'm suggesting you get clear on what's truly yours to carry versus what you've picked up along the way.

'I don't have time for soul searching'—you don't have time *not* to do this work. The cost of continuing as you are only gets higher.

If you're sitting with a blank page right now, that's normal. When we've spent years living according to other people's definitions of success, our own voice gets buried so deep we forget it exists.

Give it time. Give it space. The answers will come.

> ## What to do when you draw blanks
>
> ▸ *Move your body first:* I discovered that insight comes through motion. I'd take long walks, put on music that made me feel something, dance in my kitchen like no-one was watching. Movement unlocks what thinking can't access.
>
> ▸ *Remember when you felt truly alive:* Go back to a moment when everything felt effortless, when you felt most like yourself. What were you doing? Who were you with? How did it feel in your body? Why was this you feeling truly alive?
>
> ▸ *Study someone you admire:* Think of someone whose life makes you think 'I want what they have'—not their achievements, but their aliveness, their infectious energy and joie de vivre. What did they give themselves permission for that you haven't?
>
> ▸ *Write the scary stuff:* I wrote things I hoped no-one would ever read. The embarrassing slightly shallow stuff like a fabulous wardrobe, owning a villa in Italy, taking three months off…the life that felt too big or too different from what was expected. Write like no-one is watching…because they're not.
>
> ▸ *Sit in nature:* There's something about being surrounded by life that's just growing for the sake of growing that reminds us of what being alive actually feels like. The beauty of life. The spaciousness to just be and notice.
> Then trust whatever comes up and write that down even if it doesn't quite make sense.

> ▸ *Be patient with the process:* I drank endless cups of tea while waiting for clarity. Sometimes the answer isn't in the thinking, it's in the sitting without knowing until something true emerges.
>
> *Remember:* this isn't about creating another goal list or optimisation plan. This is about reconnecting with the part of you that knows what aliveness feels like—the part that existed before you learned you had to earn your worth through achievement.

Chris's story: When the dream job stopped being the dream

Chris was being groomed for a bigger executive role. From the outside, it looked like the perfect trajectory: senior leader, big team, high-stakes role, clear path to the top.

But Chris had lost his mojo. And, worse, he no longer wanted the role everyone assumed he was chasing.

A few life events had forced him to question everything. The next position he was supposed to want felt like a prison sentence. The reputation he'd built for being at the top of his game suddenly felt hollow. He'd achieved so much at such a young age and he wasn't sure he wanted to keep playing any more.

When we started working together, I asked him what really mattered most. The answer came immediately: his family. They were his world. And the resistance to the next level role? He believed it would cost him the time with his loved ones that he wasn't willing to sacrifice.

But something else sat underneath that fear. So we went deeper.

We explored what had shaped him. His value system. His non-negotiables. What it would look like for him to achieve without it costing his family. And then I asked him about his leadership legacy: How did he want his children to remember him?

That's when something magical happened.

He began to come alive again. He smiled more. Laughed at himself. The heaviness lifted. He came home to himself.

And here's what else happened: he realised he could still pursue the bigger role but do it his way. With clarity on what mattered most. With boundaries that protected his family. And with a renewed sense of what lit him up: creating a culture of awesome humans.

He didn't have to choose between ambition and family. He just had to redefine what success looked like when it included both.

That's what this work looks like in practice. Not revolutionary. Just real. Open. Curious. Willing to challenge yourself and dig into what really matters.

Chris is now pursuing his next role, but this time, he's doing it with clarity, intention and his family at the centre. Leading from a place of choice, not obligation. And the mojo? It's back.

What about you? How might your life change for the better?

Choosing conscious joy

The third and final part of your new definition of success is conscious joy. The element most overachievers omit entirely.

My impermanence gave me permission to finally choose joy. To focus on what lit me up. To not take myself so seriously. To let go of all the stuff that weighed me down, because I simply didn't have the time or energy for it.

I had nothing left to lose, so I could be a little wild — tend to my inner little Fleur who wanted to come out and play. I had nothing left to prove. Each day was a bonus.

I stayed curious about what drained me and what filled me. I found laughter again by not taking myself so seriously. I stayed close to people who inspired and celebrated me. I gave myself permission to not do — to just be.

I fell in love with life as it was. I aligned my life to what felt good on the inside first. I got clear that now was the time to live fully, not later.

Success that sparks joy

As a natural workaholic, my default was work first, joy later. Maybe after the next promotion. Maybe when I hit that revenue target. Maybe when everything was 'sorted'. But illness taught me something the business world never would: Later might never come.

So I made a conscious choice to weave joy into my life. Not as a reward for good behaviour, but as fuel for actually living it. I started tuning into what lit me up versus what drained me. And then (this was the hard part) I actually acted on it.

When I run workshops, I get everyone dancing. Not because I'm trying to be silly, but because the neuroscience is clear — play and movement help with learning and breakthrough thinking. And because I'd spent too many years stuck in boardrooms where joy was considered unprofessional. Getting people moving breaks down that stuffiness and reminds everyone they're human, not just their job title. I stopped taking myself so seriously and started leaning into my inner little Fleur, the one who finds delight in play and isn't afraid to look silly.

I started planning a 'look-forward-to' moment every single week without fail. Italy to watch a dear friend marry. Movies on my own because I loved the escape. Markets and preloved stores, buying things made me smile. Hanging out with Mother Nature because she always lifted my spirit. Not big things, just something that made me smile in anticipation.

I said 'no' to clients who didn't value me. Left events early when my energy was done. Chose presence over productivity when it mattered. I burned the expensive candles. Used the good china. Stopped saving joy for later because later might not come.

Here's what I discovered: Joy isn't frivolous when you're building a life worth living, it's essential.

It's what reminds you why you're working so hard in the first place. It's what keeps you connected to yourself when everything else is demanding you perform. It's what makes the tough days bearable and the good days worth savouring.

Conscious joy became my compass, not my indulgence. The thing that helped me discern what was truly worth my limited energy and what was just noise. Because success that costs you joy isn't success. It's just sophisticated suffering with impressive results.

Sequins over superwoman

So what does living fully actually look like in practice? For me, it started with sequins.

Here in Byron Bay, beige linen is practically a uniform. Natural fibres, earthy tones, effortless neutrals. And, yet, there I am on a random Tuesday morning, walking through the supermarket in sequins.

Because I can. Because life is too short for beige.

I know how it sounds. Frivolous, certainly. Here I am, fighting for my life, and I'm talking about clothes. But my wardrobe became one of my greatest joys, and I'm not apologising for it.

My passion for fashion started when I was 16. I love to dress up. Always have. But somewhere along the way, as I became the senior executive, the capable mum, the woman who had it all together, I'd started dressing for the role rather than for myself. Power suits. Polished shoes. The armour of achievement.

Then came treatment. And I made a decision: I was going to dress up for chemo.

Not in gym gear or pyjamas. I showed up in sequin sneakers and with lipstick on, looking like I was heading somewhere far more glamorous than a hospital chair. Because if I was going to sit there for hours with poison dripping into my veins, I was bloody well going to look good doing it.

Each treatment, each brutal day, I chose sparkle. Literally.

I started wearing sequins everywhere. At the supermarket. In corporate boardrooms. At home, making breakfast for the kids. Most days, I made sure I had a little on me somewhere. Something that caught the light and reminded me: Life is for living. Shine bright, darling.

It was an act of defiance. A middle finger to the illness trying to dim me. A reminder that I was not just a patient or a diagnosis, I was still the woman who loved colour and light and refusing to fade into the background.

I'd spent years wearing a superwoman cape woven from expectations, responsibilities and the crushing need to be everything to everyone. It looked impressive from the outside, but underneath? I couldn't breathe.

So I traded it in. Superwoman cape for sequins. Control for conscious joy.

The sequins weren't really about the clothes. They were about reclaiming myself. Showing up fully, even when everything felt hard. Celebrating being alive, even when life felt unbearable. Being visible and vibrant rather than shrinking into the shadow of what I thought I should be.

That's what living fully looks like: finding your version of sequins and wearing them unapologetically. Making space for what lights you up and brings you deep contentment.

Reset challenge #2: Wear the fucking sequins

So what are your sequins? What's the thing you love but won't let yourself do? The joy you've been saving for 'someday'? The part of yourself you've dimmed to fit in?

First, find your sequins: Reflect on these five questions:

1. Which moments in the last month made you feel most alive?
2. When did time disappear because you were so absorbed?
3. What activities energised you instead of draining you?
4. Where did you feel most authentically yourself?
5. What brought you real lightness and joy?

Now look at your answers and ask: When was the last time you actually prioritised these things?

Maybe it's not sequins. Maybe it's the:

1. art class you've been 'meaning to take'
2. holiday you're waiting for the 'right time' to book
3. expensive coffee you skip because the cheaper one is 'fine'
4. music you love but don't play because others don't like it
5. hobby everyone thinks is silly but makes you come alive
6. bold lipstick, the statement earrings, the thing that makes you feel like you.

Stop saving it. Stop waiting for permission. Stop dimming yourself to fit someone else's idea of appropriate. Stop postponing joy because it feels frivolous or indulgent or not quite professional enough.

Your challenge this week

Choose *one* thing from your reflections — one sequin moment, one joy you've been postponing — and do it. This week. Not someday. This week.

Wear the bold colour. Book the class. Buy the expensive coffee. Play the music loud. Use the good china. Burn the fancy candles. Do the thing that makes you feel like yourself.

Not because you've earned it. Not because it's practical. Not because anyone else will understand. Because you're alive, and that's reason enough. The real superpower isn't holding it all together while performing the role everyone expects. It's choosing to show up as yourself: fully, boldly, unapologetically.

My ambition reimagined

After figuring out what mattered to me, what I truly wanted from my life and realising that I needed to live fully, I decided to write the last legacy I wanted to be remembered for to truly anchor in my ambition. Here it is, exactly as I wrote it in 2019, imperfect and raw... As you read this, notice what lights you up and what doesn't land. Both reactions are valuable information about what *your* authentic ambition might look like.

> 1 May 2019
>
> I want my legacy to be around helping people feel that they matter and are enough just the way they are — in fact they are beyond enough, they are amazing as they are.
>
> I want to hold the mirror up, hold the space so they too can see their awesomeness, own it and really see their real potential.
>
> To do this, I need to share my story, continue to be deeply vulnerable and real, and show my character by being my true best self yet, also being messy, so I give others permission to be messy too. Walking my talk and staying real. Showing up as my true self and honouring it.

As a leader, I want to be remembered for creating unique life-changing experiences that help people realise their potential, giving generously of tools and ways to create a sustainable work life where you can live fully — not at the cost to your health or what really matters to you.

As a mother, I want to be remembered for my sense of self, being true to myself and my values, following my heart, wearing my heart on my sleeve and showing up fully as me. I want to be remembered for working hard, striving for a better life, standing up for what I believe in and how to just be without worrying about others and what they think of me — owning all of who I am, no matter what. That family is everything and love makes the world go round and can solve almost anything.

As a family member, I want to be remembered for loving unconditionally and seeing the beauty in all that is my family. To create rituals that will last over time: Sunday dinners, church on special days, sharing a meal, Sunday walks. To teach my children that home is where your family is not what you have or the roof over your head.

As a human, I want to be remembered for shining bright, despite it all. My smile, my energy, my grace, my sequins and love for fashion. My passion, my resilience, persistence, determination and my sheer grit and willingness to fight the good fight and, most of all, never giving up. To, ultimately, be the living proof that it is not what happens to you that matters but how you react to it and what you can learn from it.

As a woman leader, I want to be remembered for helping other women lift up into their bigger game and to live their best life as they so deserve. To teach them the importance of self-care, self-compassion and boundaries. To be consciously selfish to be sustainably generous in all the roles they need to show up for. To show them you don't have to have it all together and to stay connected to your sense of self always — the inner little girl needs you. To love yourself and listen to your heart.

I also want to be remembered for my joie de vivre — my joy for life. Never taking myself too seriously. My fun-loving, generous spirit. For my ability to connect with anyone and see them as them, opening my heart to them and their story, accepting them and all they bring. To honour my slightly crazy, insane, wilful self that pushes through and steps out of the norm to liven the room up or just have some fun. I want to be remembered for truly celebrating, respecting and loving life and all it has to offer.

I want to be remembered for making people feel like I care. I want to be the leader who showed up wholeheartedly. To be able to help people with the juggle of life and find ways to navigate the challenges so they honour their values, who they are and what matters to them.

I want to create a ripple effect of kindness, compassion, sustainability, self-leadership and respect

Love, Fleur
Chief heart officer of my life

When I wrote this in 2019, I thought I had months left. Maybe a year if I was lucky. I had no guarantees. None of us do.

It's taken years to realise this legacy — to actually live it rather than just write it down. And I feel profoundly lucky to have had so much extra time, time I never expected to have.

I'm grateful to still be here to share it with you now.

A few months ago, I dug out this 2019 ambition statement to share with women leaders in one of my programs. When I found it, I realised something profound: I hadn't just survived my reimagining, I had thrived because of it. I had lived fully with deep contentment. I had shown up consistently for all that life offered.

My ambition now isn't about proving myself, it's about continuing to be fully myself.

What I know to be true

- When you stop chasing other people's definition of success, something remarkable happens: Space opens up, and in that space, you finally hear your own voice telling you what you actually want from this one precious life. Not what you *should* want. Not what would *look* impressive. What actually lights you up from the inside.

- The clearer you become about what truly matters to you, the easier it is to build a life that includes you in it. These aren't just nice-to-haves or aspirational ambitions. They become your compass, shaping every decision and defining your real impact.

- Here's the truth about living fully: There will always be tension between the twinkle and the tear. Just when you think you've got it sorted, life will remind you that you're not in control. And that's where the gold lives—in that uncomfortable, messy space between what you hoped for and what actually is. Your darkest struggles aren't obstacles to success. They're the part of your growth where meaning is found.

> ✧ Once you're clear on what you truly want, it becomes your choice to make it happen. To take the steps that align your life with what you really want. To bravely claim what's yours as you so deserve.
>
> ✧ And finally—this matters more than anything—choose conscious joy. Not as a reward for later, once you've earned it. Not as an afterthought squeezed between everything else, but as an intentional way of living and leading right now. Bring play, bring lightness, bring sequins to the journey. Because this is it. This is your life and it is a long road if you don't celebrate along the way.

Reset challenge #3: Embodying success your way

Here's the thing about changing patterns that have been running your life for years: You need new practices to replace the old ones. Here's two simple ones to get you started.

1. Your weekly ambition check

At the end of every week, spend ten minutes with your journal reflecting on how you're living your reimagined ambition:

- How did I show up for myself this week?
- Where did I feel most alive and authentic?
- What brought me closer to the life I actually want?
- What did I learn that I want to remember for next week?

This isn't about productivity or achievements, it's about staying connected to what matters and course correcting as you go. Ponder what you will do differently for the week ahead, and do that.

2. Your daily sparkle

Every morning, before you look at your phone, before you check your emails, before you dive into the world's demands, ask yourself one simple question:

What do I want to do today that will light me up?

Not what you should do. Not what others expect. What do you actually want to do that will bring you joy or a sense of aliveness?

Then choose one thing and do it intentionally.

Maybe it's wearing your favourite outfit. Taking a walk without your phone. Having a proper cup of coffee instead of rushing through it. Sitting in the sun for ten minutes. Calling a friend.

These aren't achievements to tick off. They're moments of aliveness. Your sequins showing up in an ordinary day.

For the next seven days:

- *Morning:* Ask the question (What do I want to do today that will light me up?) and decide on your one thing.
- *During the day:* Actually do it (don't let it slide).
- *Evening:* Notice how it impacted your energy and how you showed up.

Start small. This isn't another thing to optimise or perfect. It's permission to let joy be part of your daily life, not something you earn after you've achieved enough.

Your ambition matters. But so does the version of you who's pursuing it.

✨ Glittering truths ✨

If you only remember three things from this chapter, make them these:

1. Get crystal clear on what matters most to you

Not what should matter, but what actually does matter. Your values aren't just nice words on a wall, they're your decision-making filter for how you live and lead. When you know what you stand for, you stop wasting mental energy on what doesn't align. You stop chasing definitions of success that were handed to you and start building one that's authentically yours. The clarity comes from asking the hard question: If this is it, what do I truly want my life to be?

2. Reimagine your ambition so it includes you in the equation

You don't need to shrink your ambition, you need to reset the way you pursue it. Authentic ambition energises rather than depletes. It's connected to your values, your strengths, your genuine desire for impact. Success that costs you your health, your joy, your relationships, your sense of self isn't success at all, it's just sophisticated self-destruction with impressive outcomes. Your ambition can be powerful *and* sustainable when it serves your whole life, not just your CV.

3. Living fully isn't something you earn after achievement

It's a choice you make right now. Conscious joy is not frivolous, it's fuel. Stop saving the good china. Burn the expensive candles. Wear the sequins on Tuesday. Choose joy today not when everything is sorted, not after the next promotion, not when you've proven yourself one more time. Because 'later' isn't guaranteed. The life you're saving things for? This is it.

9

PILLAR TWO: LEAD WITH IMPACT

How to create real impact without losing yourself in the process

'Mastering others is strength. Mastering yourself is true power.'

—Lao Tzu

When life tests you twice

I thought I was done. Done with treatments, done with uncertainty, done with my body betraying me. I'd made my peace with living with a chronic illness. I'd found my rhythm, my acceptance, my new normal. I had done my inner work to reset.

And then life decided I wasn't quite finished learning yet.

Another storm. Another moment of surrender. Another choice about how I'd show up.

It was a regular mammogram now that I was over 40. I was heading to New Zealand for work so managed to squeeze in the time to get it done. I was lying on the radiology bed after my mammogram and the radiographer went to go and get the doctor to check 'something'. I held my breath. Surely not. The doctor came back and asked if I had an oncologist. I replied I have every other 'gist' — immunologist, gynaecologist, endocrinologist, urologist, ophthalmologist... Gulp. *We think you need an urgent biopsy. Can you get this done when you get back from your trip?*

I booked it in. I was madly googling 'breast cancer' as I left the radiography rooms, saying to myself that there is no way I would be that unlucky.

Between the biopsy and getting the results, I had my team Christmas lunch. Everyone was in good spirits while I pretended — smiling on the outside, a bundle of nerves within, knowing that in a few hours I'd have the news.

I got to the doctor's clinic and was told to go straight in. My doctor Martine looked up with sad eyes. Breast cancer. Immediate surgery needed. My immune-compromised body was a party waiting to go off.

I stumbled to the car before losing it completely. Called my hubby Pete. 'Come home and we'll deal with it', he said, shocked but not surprised. On the 45-minute drive home, I played the saddest music, sobbing uncontrollably, processing the reality ahead. Mind racing with what-ifs coming faster than my speed limit.

The anger: *How bloody unfair. What had I done to deserve this? I mean WTF!*

Pulling into the driveway, I felt the weight of how my news would shatter my family. My mask sliding back up. I wasn't ready to speak it out loud — that would make it real. I needed more time. I pulled myself together, packing down my flooding emotions as I walked up the steps to my front door, fine mask on, eyes still swollen, yet brave smile as I walked in the door. My heart sank as my kids hugged me. How would I even tell them. Fark!

Chronic illness had come for me twice. The first time, it broke me. The second time, it met a different woman.

This time it met a woman who knew the difference between surviving and thriving, between enduring and healing. Who understood that the only way forward is through. So I braced myself, stood with feet on the ground, ready for anything. I had proven I was stronger than I imagined. I had been incredibly resilient despite it all.

And I was reminded yet again:

> It's not what happens to you but how you respond that matters.

In that moment, while despair and defeat dominated my thoughts, I needed to make intentional choices about how I was going to show up. Not just for this diagnosis, but for my team, my family, my life. I had to integrate the powerful lessons I'd learned about vulnerability and strength. Face the reality of living in a body I couldn't control and recognise it had become my greatest teacher.

This became the ultimate test of what I thought I knew about leadership. And here's what I discovered: By having nothing left to lose, I became the best leader I'd ever been because I was wiser than before, having done the inner reset. I had no choice but to lead intentionally.

Choosing with intention

Leading with impact—in your work, in your relationships, in your life—is about intentional choices. Daily, deliberate decisions about:

- what you focus on
- what you model for others and yourself
- how you respond versus react
- how you hold yourself throughout your day
- what strength looks like when you don't have the answers.

When crisis hits, these intentional choices shape how you navigate yourself and the people you love through whatever lies ahead.

To lead and live with impact means accepting a hard truth: You can't do everything. You have to make conscious choices about what truly matters—at work, at home, in your relationships, for yourself—and recognise the rest is simply noise.

The person who creates real impact has clarity and perspective. They respond, not react. They dial down the busy, let go of the worry, get crystal clear about what matters.

It's about being hyper-disciplined every day. Disciplined about the choices you make as you show up for yourself, your work, your people, your life. Having the courage to be self-aware enough to separate what's important from what's not. Recognising how you show up impacts everyone around you—and yourself most of all.

I learned this the hard way, by having no choice but to get ruthlessly clear about what mattered and what didn't. When you're operating on limited energy and borrowed time, you can't afford to waste yourself on noise.

That clarity changed everything, and you don't need a diagnosis to get it.

Reset challenge #4: Your intentional choices audit

Take ten minutes and answer these questions honestly about how they apply across all areas of your life:

- What truly matters for the impact you want to create? (At work? In your relationships? For yourself? For your loved ones?) List three to five things in total. If you list more, you're not being honest about impact.
- What's on your plate that's simply noise? Be ruthless. What are you doing at work and in life out of habit, guilt or fear, and not because it creates impact?
- What's one behaviour you need to let go of this week that's costing you high impact? (The meeting you don't need to attend? The commitment you said 'yes' to out of guilt? The perfectionism that's exhausting you? The relationship that drains you?)
- What's one intentional choice you'll make this week to create real impact? Not 'try to make', will make. At work, at home, for yourself. One choice. This week.

Your audit isn't about adding more to your plate. It's about getting crystal clear on what deserves your limited energy (in your work, your relationships, your life) and having the courage to let the rest go. Because how you lead others and how you lead your life? Same energy. Same choices. Same impact.

The three-month experiment that changed my life

I'd already taken significant leave from my role, so could only afford a short amount of time off. My sick leave was in significant deficit.

I returned to work two weeks after completing radiation treatment. I was wiped beyond words, yet I had to keep showing up. I needed to lead others while running on empty.

As I returned to work utterly spent, my line manager said something that completely shifted my world:

What if you tried doing less and just being the leader?

This one simple question that made me question everything I thought I knew about leadership. I sat down and decided that I needed to make some intentional choices about how I would lead as I recovered:

- *Put in less effort:* I showed up holding it light, doing as little efforting as possible. My energy tank was empty. I worked shorter days, walking out at 4 pm without guilt, knowing I needed rest to keep showing up.
- *Do less, done well:* My to-do list went from overwhelming to intentional. One to two priorities per week. That's it. Less done excellently created more impact than everything done adequately. This was the hardest shift for an overachiever, but it was the most transformative.
- *Ask for help and be okay with not fixing:* I accepted I couldn't be the fixer in every room. I practised asking one question: 'What do you think your options are?' Then watched as they took ownership.
- *Open office hours:* My team needed to know when they could bounce things off me and get support so I created a regular time daily that allowed my team to drop in. I picked my highest energy time so I could give them my full attention without distractions.
- *Presence as power:* I leaned into being present to what my team needed, showing up for meetings and consciously leaving with no actions, pointing and directing like a maestro of an orchestra. I focused on what I could control, which was

> my thoughts, feelings and actions. Showing up authentically
> as me from moment to moment.

So, I bravely stepped into the unknown, holding it light, doing less and being more. Even sharing this with you now, I can feel my anxiety rise. I was so scared to dip my toe into this new way of being.

And here's what happened...

I didn't feel the usual guilt of never doing enough. My team lifted up, they took up the space I had created for them to lead, they felt truly empowered, and I felt like I was being the leader I was meant to be.

I ended each day early with energy in my tank, knowing that my team had whatever drama of the day in hand. I showed up like this for three months, not feeling guilty about not doing enough, liberated by the freedom of less pressure and space to recover.

And here's the thing, I made more impact!

That three-month experiment changed everything. I discovered there were actually two ways I could show up as a leader: both delivered excellence, but one nearly destroyed me while the other set me free. One was sustainable, the other was survivable — but only for so long.

That three-month experiment taught me something crucial: Intentional choices weren't just nice ideas, they were the difference between surviving and thriving. Between performing leadership and embodying it. Between leading at any cost and leading with sustainable impact.

Achieving sustainable excellence

Leading with impact requires understanding what excellence looks like for you. It's about setting yourself up to create real impact with the knowledge of what it means for you to perform well and sustainably. To do so in a way that energises rather than depletes you. And catching when you default back into your old, learned ways of performing at the cost of you, and resetting.

Here's what I discovered about myself (and what you need to know about yourself): There are actually two ways you can achieve excellence, but only one is sustainable.

I started getting curious about my energy patterns, when I performed at my best, what it felt like from the inside. What kicked me into overdrive versus what kept me in flow. And I realised there were ultimately two states of being for me. So typical — I'm nothing if not black and white in how I show up.

But here's what became crystal clear: I could perform with excellence in both states, yet one felt like I was in my zone while the other felt like I was in overdrive. One was sustainable. One was slowly killing me.

I've termed them my *high impact state* versus my *high cost state*.

High impact state

My high impact state is me operating from clarity and intention, showing up from my wise mind, not my 'go harder, do more' brain. I know my limits and trust my lived experience.

I make decisions in alignment with my purpose, not under pressure. I show up authentically without efforting hard or over-proving, creating generous space for others.

Whatever I'm doing feels aligned with who I truly am. I achieve and create impact in ways that energise rather than deplete me, building something meaningful while staying whole.

I operate from clarity, not chaos. I show up as myself, not some version I think people need. Me doing me creates permission for others to do them.

I consciously dial down life's noise and focus on what matters, being present, trusting I'm exactly where I need to be. There's space for play, for being silly. I lean into struggle moments knowing I still have much to learn.

I do less but do it well, caring less about what doesn't matter. Simply living and leading fully — one day at a time.

Wise mind leading, inner Fleur playing, magnificence owned.

High cost state

I'm in a high cost state when I wake with this big invisible foot on my back pushing me harder, that quiet whisper: 'do more, go harder, you're not enough'.

I slip my mask on, pretending everything's fine while achieving and falling apart inside. I'm operating from my over-functioning mind while my body screams at me to slow down, but stopping isn't optional.

Time feels like it's running out. Every decision feels urgent as I effort through everything, rushing and talking fast because it's all a blur.

I'm overperforming, efforting hard yet feeling the energy drain like I'm walking with concrete boots. My brain's in a fog, my body a heavy weight trudging through the day. I'm over-polishing everything, taking twice as long because I'm too tired to think clearly.

I've abandoned my sense of self, forgetting the hard-earned lessons that cost me my health. My inner critic is tutting at me as I betray what I know is true.

By evening, I'm comforting myself with salt and vinegar chips and vino, doomscrolling, feeling lesser than, getting judgy and lost in comparison. Table 9.1 compares these excellence states.

Table 9.1 Two excellence states

High impact state: Sustainable excellence	High cost state: Excellence at any cost
You operate at a sustainable pace that fuels you rather than drains you.	You push harder even though you know there is a cost to your health, focus, energy and relationships.
You're clear on what truly matters: focus is sharp, decisions are clear, and noise is filtered out.	Everything feels urgent—you're reacting, firefighting and decision fatigue clouds your judgement.
Boundaries hold under pressure. You know what you need to show up as your best self and know your limits too.	Boundaries collapse. You say 'yes' to any requests, overcommit and overpromise, and let other people's priorities run your day.

(continued)

Table 9.1 Two excellence states (*cont'd*)

High impact state: Sustainable excellence	High cost state: Excellence at any cost
You're intentional in how you show up: present, energised and deliberate in your impact, catching yourself when you need to steady your overdrive.	Default mode: You run on autopilot, driven by unrelenting standards, fear of dropping the ball, and your inner critic is the boss of you.
Work feels purposeful. You're motivated, excited, energised and delivering real impact.	Work feels like a grind. You're depleted, scattered, everything takes you longer and you're second-guessing yourself and whether it is worth it.
You respond rather than react. You choose your moves and ignore what doesn't really matter.	Reacting without pause or regulation. You let the moment dictate your moves, you're emotionally dysregulated, acting out of character for you and creating a sense of stress and panic around you.
You operate from clarity, a sense of self and grounded confidence.	You operate from pressure, emptiness, baseline fatigue and self-doubt.
Leader by intention.	Leader by performance.

You can deliver exceptional results from your high impact state or from your high cost state. Both work in the short term, but only one protects your energy, your health and your ability to keep showing up as the leader you want to be.

In *high impact*, you're the leader you want to be: focused, grounded, true to how you intend to show up for yourself and others, delivering value and impact without losing yourself.

In *high cost*, you look like you're performing at your peak, but underneath, you're burning through energy, health and joy just to keep up.

Table 9.2 is crystal clear about the difference:

Table 9.2 Leader by intention vs performance

Leader by intention	Leader by performance
Knows what matters and focuses there.	Tries to do everything and please everyone.
Sets and holds boundaries, even under pressure.	Drops boundaries when the heat is on.
Chooses responses instead of reactions.	Reacts to urgency and noise.
Works at a sustainable pace that fuels energy and clarity.	Runs on unrelenting standards and self-pressure.
Leads with purpose, presence and impact.	Measures worth by output, not by value or impact.

Here's what became very clear to me during those three months: I wasn't just switching between good days and bad days, I was switching between two completely different operating systems. And once I could name them, I could consciously choose between them.

So I made intentional choices about what mattered. I practised showing up in my high impact state. I let myself be magnificently me because I'd learned that through authenticity, real influence and connection can be found.

Reset challenge #5: Your excellence states deep dive

Grab your journal. Let's get curious what it looks like for you to show up in high-impact mode versus when you're in high cost mode.

First, recall a moment when you were operating as your best leader self — creating real impact without exhausting yourself and being authentically you. What was happening? How did you feel? What was the environment like? Just write — don't overthink it.

Your high impact state

The experience

- What does it look, feel and sound like when you're operating with high impact?
- How do you show up differently? What do you notice from within?
- How do others experience you when you're in this state?

The access

- What gets you into this state?
- What knocks you out of it?

Your high cost state

The experience

- What does it look, feel and sound like when you're operating at any cost?
- How do you show up differently? What do you notice happening inside?
- How do others experience you when you're in this state?

The access

- What triggers you into this state?
- What are your early warning signs that you've slipped into high cost mode?

Your reset challenge

- What did you notice about the differences between your two states?
- What can you do to stay in your high impact state more consistently?

- What are one to three actions you can take as a result of this deeper awareness to help you stay in high impact state more?
- What do you need to remember about yourself when you're stuck in the wrong state?

Relearning this lesson again

Just this week, while writing this very chapter, I was reminded that sustainable excellence isn't a destination, it's a daily choice. And sometimes, even when you know better, you choose the old way.

I was tested beyond my limits by a client who, while on a call with me, was texting my senior client that I hadn't delivered on my scope of work — not directly confronting me about what she actually needed. While it was a small issue that I could easily solve, I felt betrayed. My 'not good enough' trigger had been activated, and I was off to the races.

So I doubled down. I worked through the night, angry and wired, sleeping only for three hours. By 8 am the next day, I had done what would take a normal human a week's worth of work — and more. I was fired up, my chest tight, my mind was racing with that familiar buzz of adrenaline that feels productive but is actually destructive.

It was a masterclass in high cost state: the invisible foot on my back, the concrete boots dragging me through each task, the mask firmly in place while falling apart inside. I put in all my self-regulation practices to try and cool my over-efforting system, now in complete overload, yet I couldn't slow down.

I spiralled for another few days. Working hard, not sleeping, not eating, not resting — just performing to prove my worth. The emotions were flooding me, my inner critic was on full volume. I reached out for help to soothe me, but nothing was working.

To reset, I had to literally put myself to bed the morning I was meant to run a workshop, cancelling everything so I could actually show up again as my authentic self and walk my talk, rather than perform from depletion.

It took me another seven days to come off the high cost state and really reset. Daily practices to slow down, calm my farm, and constant catching of my high cost behaviours to regulate back to my high impact state, so I could write this book.

The irony wasn't lost on me. Here I was, writing about sustainable excellence while completely abandoning everything I know that works. But that's the thing about this work, it's not about perfection. It's about recognising the warning signs, catching the triggers and then focusing on what you know works to reset to your high impact state.

Even when you know better, sometimes you need the reminder that the old way will always be there waiting. The difference now is how quickly you can catch yourself and choose a more sustainable path again.

Being magnificently you

Once you've intentionally chosen how you want to show up, something shifts.

You stop trying to be the leader everyone expects and start being the leader only you can be. The one who brings your whole self, not just the polished, professional parts. The one who leads from their values, strengths, their genuine care for people. The one who doesn't apologise for the qualities that make them different.

This is what being magnificently *you* looks like. And it's not about perfection or performance, it's about presence. Authenticity. The courage to stop hiding who you are and start leading from it — at work, at home, in every room you walk into.

The more yourself you become and the more vulnerable you are, the more influential you are and the greater the connection you have with others.

Read that again. Think about it for a moment. It was a real game changer for me and how I show up, not just at work, but with my kids, my friends, in every relationship that matters.

Showing up more fully as my authentic self (as I was too exhausted or unwell to be anything but) — being vulnerable, not having it together all the time, owning who I am through my mindset work on radical acceptance, and operating from grounded confidence — I became a better influencer for impact in every area of my life.

Vulnerability isn't weakness. It's competitive advantage. And it's less exhausting than performing.

When you're self-aware and operating as yourself, you navigate tough moments better. You make better decisions under pressure. You recover faster from setbacks. You inspire confidence instead of anxiety — in your team when things get wobbly, in your kids when life feels uncertain, in yourself when you're facing the unknown.

When you stop performing and start embodying authenticity, people feel it. Your team trusts you more. Your kids relax around you. Your relationships deepen. Because people don't connect with perfect, they connect with real.

The research[34] backs this up: Authentic leadership creates 76 per cent higher engagement and stronger trust. But here's what the research doesn't tell you — it works everywhere. With your team, yes, but also with your partner, your kids, your friends. Authenticity creates connection. Performance creates distance.

A study in *Harvard Business Review*[35] found that people at high-trust companies (in comparison to people at low-trust companies) also report:

- 74 per cent less stress
- 106 per cent more energy at work
- 50 per cent higher productivity
- 13 per cent fewer sick days

- 29 per cent more satisfaction with their lives
- 40 per cent less exhaustion.

When I have felt truly self-certain, operating as my high-impact best self, and been in a supportive environment where I am valued, I have found coming from my true self has allowed me to influence rooms full of people. It is like an energy that ripples into the room creating a sense of truth and trust where people simply want to believe in you and your point of view.

But it's not just boardrooms. It's the dinner table when your teenager finally opens up because you stopped performing 'perfect parent' and started being real. It's the difficult conversation with your partner where dropping the defence creates breakthrough. It's every moment where you choose presence over performance.

It's those moments when you abandon your PowerPoint slides mid-presentation because you can sense you have lost the room. You pivot away from your script and just have a conversation not a presentation. You know these moments. When you surrender the script and just be you — people lean in. At work. At home. Everywhere.

Self-certainty foundations

Here's what I learned about showing up as magnificently me: it's built on three foundations. With nothing left to lose, I made a conscious choice to work on my self-belief, not just as a leader, but as a whole person. There were three core areas that became my foundation for what it means to be self-certain:

1. *Grounded confidence*: Owning all that you are and trusting your judgement at work, at home, in every decision you make.
2. *Operating from your true self*: Being you without trying to be anyone else whether you're in a boardroom or your living room.

3. *Life on your own terms*: Not benchmarking against others or seeking validation from anyone, including your boss, your peers, your loved ones or society.

These aren't just leadership principles, they're life principles. The way you show up at work is the way you show up everywhere. And the moment you start being magnificently you in one area, it ripples into all the others.

From my experience, the person who creates real impact (at work and in life) does so, not in the good times, but in the messy, uncertain times. When change forces you to step up. When your team is watching to see if you'll crumble or show up as your authentic self despite it all. When your kids need you to hold steady and be real with them, showing both vulnerability and strength when you are not sure what lies ahead. When you hold space boldly, when you're navigating your struggles with grace — that's when they see what's possible. When you show up anyway, messy and real and fully present — that's leadership. When you choose truth over performance, even when it's uncomfortable: at work, at home, in every hard moment.

And within us, the same is true. It's the messy, hardest parts of life that transform us. The moments when everything falls apart and we have to decide: Will I pretend or will I be real? Will I perform strength or will I embody it?

That intentional choice to show up as your magnificent, flawed, uncertain, courageous self is what separates people who create real impact from people who just get through the day.

Here are the signs you're leading from your true self:

- You feel lighter with greater clarity, not heavier with more pressure.
- You have energy after key moments, not depletion.
- You can ask for help without feeling like you're failing.

- People say things like 'I trust your judgement' not just 'great job'.
- People are more willing to admit their mistakes.
- You're comfortable saying 'I don't know' and finding answers together.
- You stop needing external validation to feel confident about decisions.
- Your influence grows without you having to work harder for it.
- Your relationships deepen because people finally see the real you.
- You stop exhausting yourself maintaining a version of you that isn't real.

This is what being magnificently you looks like in real life. Not perfect. Not polished. Not performing. Just powerfully, authentically, courageously you in every room, every relationship, every moment that matters.

Naz's story: When authenticity became an advantage

Naz was standing at a crossroads. As a senior leader being tapped for a bigger role, this was the kind of opportunity she'd worked for years to earn.

But she was watching other leaders at that next level sacrifice everything for the job. Their personal lives. Their health. Their sense of self. And she was questioning: Is this what ambition costs?

Coming from a large family that mattered deeply to her, wanting to be the best mum she could be, needing space to take care of herself—she was questioning whether pursuing her ambition was worth it. Maybe she should just stay where she was.

The company's definition of senior leadership felt like a performance she'd have to maintain. She'd made assumptions about what it meant to lead at that level, and believed she'd have to become someone she wasn't. That she'd have to give up her sense of self to be that leader.

Then, in one of my leadership program workshops, she had her 'aha' moment.

She realised she didn't have to be anyone but herself. That authenticity and vulnerability drove connection and influence, not polish and performance. That real leadership was about being herself, not performing a version of herself.

So she got serious about what that really meant. What choices did she need to make if she were going to take on the bigger role? What did leading as her authentic self actually look like in her behaviours and actions?

She bravely took the promotion but on her terms.

She decided she needed to take care of herself along the way to be able to show up and create impact. That she didn't need to say 'yes' to everything. That she could push back and manage others' expectations by communicating what mattered. She got clear, focused and present on what impact looked like for her, not what it was supposed to look like.

Here's what happened.

People started commenting on how well she looked. Yes, she'd been to the gym more often, but more than that, she was holding herself differently. Lighter. More grounded.

People began tuning into her point of view more in critical conversations. Her influence grew without her having to work harder for it.

She felt more alive and capable at work and at home.

She gave herself permission to leave at a reasonable hour, knowing that rest and family time allowed her to show up sustainably.

She made space for things that helped her perform at her best rather than leaving them to last.

And she began making real impact. Not the performing kind. The authentic kind.

That's what leading from your true self looks like in practice. Not perfect. Not polished. Just real. Just her. Just sustainable.

When your brain fights back

As you begin to show up as your authentic, confident self, your overachiever brain won't go quietly. It's been running the show for years, keeping you 'safe' through performance and perfection, so expect some push back when you start unveiling the real you and letting go of the masks.

Here are three internal challenges that came up for me when I began operating as my authentic best leader self and how to navigate them.

1. But what if I'm wrong?

This one had me in knots. Wrong about *what*, exactly? Your values? Your instincts? Your worth as a human being?

Here's what I learned: There's a massive difference between being wrong about facts and being wrong about who you are. You might get a strategy wrong, make a mistake or make a decision that doesn't pan out. That's data, not identity.

The reframe that changed everything: 'I might be wrong about this decision, but I'm not wrong about my values or my worth.'

2. What if people don't like the real me?

Ah, the leadership loneliness myth. The story that says if people see who you really are (aka flawed, uncertain and not having all the answers), they'll lose respect for you.

Here's the truth no-one tells overachievers: You're already lonely. Performing for approval creates connection to your mask, not to you. Quality connections beat quantity approval every single time.

The people who matter will respect your authenticity. The people who don't respect it? They were never your people anyway.

3. How do I maintain authority while being vulnerable?

This was my biggest fear. I thought vulnerability meant weakness, that showing uncertainty would undermine my credibility.

But here's what I discovered: Vulnerability isn't about oversharing or having no boundaries. It's about having the courage to show up fully with uncertainties, wobbly moments and all. It's about being real within professional boundaries.

Authentic authority isn't about having all the answers, it's about being brave enough to say 'I don't know, let's figure it out together', and meaning it.

Your brain will keep trying to pull you back to the safety of performance. When it does, remember: The only thing scarier than being seen is never being known.

What I know to be true

✧ When you show up from your high impact state, with intentional choices, authentic presence and clarity about what matters, everything shifts. Not just at work, but everywhere. For you and for everyone around you.

✧ You'll have the energy to keep showing up. The clarity to make decisions that align with your values. The courage to be real instead of perfect. And people will feel it. Your team

(continued)

will lean in differently. Your kids will open up more. Your relationships will deepen. Because people connect with real, not perfect.

✧ You create real impact not by doing more, but by being more intentional about how you show up. By operating from your high impact state consistently, catching yourself when you slip into high cost, and resetting before you spiral.

Here's what surprised me most: being authentic takes less energy than performing does. When you stop maintaining the mask, you free up enormous capacity for actual living—and leading.

✧ You don't need to be utterly depleted to make intentional choices about how you show up. You just need courage. The courage to admit when you're in high cost state. The courage to show up authentically rather than perfectly. The courage to trust that who you are is exactly who people need you to be.

This is about becoming more fully yourself: at work, at home, everywhere.

I discovered my two excellence states because I had no energy left to pretend. I learned to create impact because I had nothing left to prove. I became my most influential when I stopped performing and started being real.

And I'm still practising. Seven years into this work, I still slip into high cost state. The difference? I catch it faster. I reset quicker. I've built practices that bring me back.

✧ *You have a choice I didn't think I had:* You can choose to operate from high impact before your body forces you to. Don't wait until you're running on empty. Don't wait until you collapse. Don't wait until the cost becomes unbearable. Start now. Choose intentionally. Recognise your states. Show up authentically.

The person you want to be? That's who you already are when you stop trying to be who you think you should be. The people who matter? They're waiting for the real you to show up.

Reset challenge #6: Your weekly high-impact reset

You've learned about intentional choices, excellence states and being magnificently you. Now it's time to live it.

Every Sunday evening or Monday morning, take 30 minutes to design your week from high-impact, integrating the three practices from this chapter into how you actually show up.

This practice is like a religion for me as it sets the intention up for how I want to create impact for the week ahead and get what matters done. I usually sit somewhere I enjoy, like my favourite cafe or perhaps outside in nature, and do this before I get swept up in the week.

Intentional choices

- *This week's focus:* What is the focus for the week ahead? What am I going to put my attention, time and energy to?
- *Priority filter:* What are the top three goals that I want to accomplish above everything else this week to create real impact?
- *My five most important tasks:* What are the most important tasks that I must get done over everything else this week?

Excellence state design

- *High impact state:* What would operating from high impact look like this week (name it specifically)?
- *Weekly self-care habits:* What are the one to five core self-care habits I want to stick to, knowing what my week ahead looks like? How can I set myself up for high impact this week?
- *Feeling intention:* How do I want to feel this week? Pick an emotion that will centre you.

Being magnificently you

- *My one commitment:* What is the one action I will commit to this week to stay in high-impact mode consistently and show up authentically?
- *My one look-forward-to moment:* What will bring you joy this week? What's your reward? What lights you up?

Intentional diary management

Use your diary to intentionally shape your week ahead to make sure you deliver on your priorities and your most important tasks around your existing commitments.

- *Intentional time management:* Taking into consideration your energy and priorities, what do you need to move to another week (or not do at all)? How are you going to make time for what matters based on your diary?
- *Meeting audit:* Which meetings actually need you vs could be handled differently: either delegated, declined or moved to another date?
- *Boundary protection:* What boundaries do you need to set to stay in your zone of excellence? What do you need to say 'no' to this week to focus on what matters? When do you

need to start and finish your day to ensure you sustain your high impact state?

- *Focused work:* Book in the focused work you need to do to ensure you meet your number one most important task of the week. Then begin to plan in other focused work to reach your goals.

Weekly check-in

At the end of the week, put aside 30 minutes to self-reflect on how your week played out. Make it a meeting with yourself on a Friday. Ask yourself the following questions, consciously focusing more on how you showed up than your outcomes:

- What worked well this week? How did you feel?
- What are you grateful for this week?
- What was this week's best moment?
- What were your wins this week?
- What is one lesson you learned this week? Reflect on the choices you made that really helped you show up in your high impact state. Perhaps reflect on when you wobbled out. What would you do differently next time?
- Think of one word to sum up the week.
- What are three things you didn't get done but must do next week (making sure you don't forget when Monday swings around)?
- Choose one productivity habit to work on next week that perhaps you didn't do this week.
- Rate your week's impact. How did you go on a scale of 1–10, with 1 being a high cost week for you and 10 being high impact (nailed it!).

Download the one-page weekly planner from fleurmarks.com.au and make this practice part of how you lead with impact.

✨ Glittering truths ✨

If you only remember three things from this chapter, make them these:

1. There are two ways to achieve excellence, and only one is sustainable

You can deliver exceptional results from your high impact state or your high cost state. Both work in the short term, but only one protects your energy, your health and your ability to keep showing up as the person you want to be. Learn to recognise which state you're in. Name it. Then choose intentionally. Because the difference between the two isn't just how you feel, it's whether you can sustain the brilliance you're capable of in your work, your relationships and your life.

2. Your authenticity is your influence

The more yourself you become and the more vulnerable you are, the more influential you are and the greater the connection you have with others. At work, yes, but also at home, with your kids, with your partner, with every person who matters. Vulnerability isn't weakness, it's competitive advantage. When you stop performing and start being real, people feel it. They trust you more. They lean in. They connect. The shift multiplies impact from 'How do I look?' to 'How do I serve?'

3. Real impact is forged in uncertainty, not certainty

The moments that define you aren't the polished wins, they're the messy, uncertain moments when everything feels like it's falling apart. When your team needs you to hold steady. When your kids need you to be real about your struggles. When life demands you show up as your magnificent, flawed, courageous self instead of the version you think people need. That's when people watch. That's when they decide whether to trust you. That's when real impact is made at work and at home.

10

PILLAR THREE: EXCELLENCE WITHOUT EXHAUSTION

Discovering that working smarter isn't just better than working harder, it's the only way to sustain brilliance

'We are what we repeatedly do. Excellence, then, is not an act, but a habit.'

—*Aristotle*

Self-full to be self-less

My teenage daughter said to me one day, *Mum, you have to be self-full to be self-less.* I stopped mid-sentence. She'd been watching me juggle a senior role while parenting her through my illness, and she'd seen what I couldn't yet admit: I was giving from an empty cup.

Later that night, I pondered what this actually meant. It felt selfish even thinking about it. How different would my life be if I felt truly self-full?

As an overachiever, your immediate reaction is probably: 'That sounds selfish.'

I know. Because that was my first thought too.

It was so far from my natural operating system, I didn't even know where to begin. For me, it was about putting my self-care first so I could be of service to others. It was about making sure I did something most days that lit me up and brought a smile to my face. It was about being okay with going to the gym and starting work at 9.30 am (instead of my usual 8 am) after kid drop off. It was creating space to think and plan, to be intentional about what excellence looked like for me every day. Recognising and accepting my limits as well as honouring them so I finished the day with some fuel left in the tank and could be present to my kids and stay well for longer. Being intentional about what my one look-forward-to moment was at the end of the week to keep me going when I was at the end of my endurance.

It was the deep commitment to be self-full so I could be self-less. And to make sure my day, week, month honoured that first.

And when I practised this way of operating, my life changed. Here's the thing: I actually had more to give by being self-full!

For example, if I tended to that one important thing I needed to progress to feel satisfied, or made sure I did one thing each day that filled my cup, it created space in my diary so I had more capacity to be present. It shattered everything I thought I knew about selfishness.

Living self-full

But self-fullness required me to practise self-compassion first — and that was the hardest part.

Dr. Kristin Neff's groundbreaking research[33] on self-compassion reveals that people who practise genuine self-care (not selfish indulgence, but authentic self-attunement) actually become more generous, not less. Her studies show that self-compassionate people have lower cortisol levels, better emotional regulation and increased capacity for empathy. The guilt we feel about 'being selfish' actually depletes the very resources we need to care for others sustainably.

Self-compassion, Neff discovered, has three core components:

1. *Self-kindness vs self-judgement:* being kind to myself when I wobbled out or made mistakes or ran out of energy rather than using it as evidence that I wasn't 'good enough'
2. *Common humanity vs isolation:* sharing my struggles and vulnerabilities about how I really felt rather than pretending I was 'not that sick'
3. *Mindfulness vs over-identification with struggle:* spending time each day mindfully planning what a self-full day looked like and catching when I went into high cost impact state.

But self-compassion wasn't just a nice idea for me, it became a survival skill. Here's what those three components actually looked like when I was fighting for my life:

Self-kindness meant changing the voice in my head. When I woke up exhausted after a rough night of treatment side effects, instead of berating myself with 'You're so weak, just push through', I'd say, 'Your body fought cancer cells all night. Of course you're tired. What do you actually need right now?'

Self-kindness wasn't fluffy affirmations, it was speaking to myself the way I'd speak to someone I loved who was going through hell.

Common humanity meant finally admitting I was struggling — not just to myself, but to others. The first time I told my team 'I need help' instead of 'I've got this', something shifted. Turns out, I wasn't alone. A lot of them were struggling too, they were just waiting for permission to be human.

Sharing my struggles didn't make me weaker in their eyes, it made me real. And it gave them permission to stop pretending they had it all together too.

Mindfulness became my early warning system. I started checking in with myself throughout the day: 'How does my body feel right now? What's my energy actually at? What do I need?' Not what I should need according to my to-do list — what I actually needed to stay functional. That simple check-in practice (pausing three times a day to ask 'How am I really?') caught me before I tipped too far into depletion.

When we're truly self-full, we operate from abundance, not depletion. We have more to give because we're not giving from empty.

I decided to surrender to this idea. Each day I asked myself: 'How would I fill my cup today to be self-full?' I'd pick one doable thing before anything else. That might be reading my book in bed before jumping up to conquer the day. Gym before work and starting my work day at 9.30 am without guilt. Taking actual lunch breaks. Having nice coffee from the cafe, not crappy workstation brew.

Here's what happened over the weeks: *I had more to give*. I didn't stress as much. I smiled more. I felt fuller inside, taking care of myself first, then giving more because I had more in my cup to offer.

It wasn't selfish, it was strategic, and it transformed everything I thought I knew about sustainable performance.

Self-fullness isn't optional. It's the foundation everything else is built on. Without it, your boundaries collapse, your practices fail and you're back to performing excellence at the cost of yourself.

Braving bold boundaries

After working on self-fullness, I realised something uncomfortable: I had a serious boundary problem. And the only person who could fix it was me.

I'd spent years abandoning my own boundaries the moment someone needed me or the pressure was on, and it was exhausting me.

I started with holding myself to my own boundaries, which I tended to surrender the moment someone needed me or the pressure was on. I needed to stop abandoning myself as this was one of the main causes of my exhaustion. I knew I tended to surrender my boundaries when I was triggered or exhausted.

You know the pattern. You say 'yes' to someone, immediately regret it, and then find yourself wondering how on earth you ended up taking on more, staying late to get it done while everyone else has gone home.

I explored a bit deeper behind what was driving my boundary drop. I asked myself several questions to get clear on why I was consistently surrendering my boundaries:

- What was the deeper fear that sat behind me giving up the boundary?
- Why was holding this boundary important to me?
- What actions could I put in place to hold that boundary that I was not doing?
- How will I hold myself accountable for this boundary?

The deepest fear making it difficult for me to hold my boundaries sat with my belief systems from Part I — from people-pleasing, wanting to be enough, to be valued and to belong.

So I got clear on the areas of my life where boundaries would be held, and which areas were more flexible.

How boundaries quietly disappear

Boundaries don't collapse all at once. Researchers Henry Cloud and John Townsend[36] mapped out how they erode in three predictable stages:

Stage 1: The flexible boundaries (The gateway)

This is where it started for me. Small compromises that seemed reasonable:

- *'I'll* just *push through the day with no real breaks and rest later'* (physical needs became negotiable).
- *'I'll* just *check emails while watching TV to stay on top of things'* (presence becomes divided).
- *'I'll* just *work a bit late tonight'* (time boundaries soften).

Stage 2: The important boundaries (The acceleration)

Then the stakes got higher:

- Working through weekends became normal.
- Taking calls during family time became expected.
- Saying 'no' became impossible.

By the time I realised what was happening, I'd trained everyone (including myself) that my boundaries were negotiable.

Stage 3: The critical boundaries (The crisis)

This is where I ended up:

- Ignoring severe fatigue (health becomes expendable).
- Pushing through warning signs my body was sending (body signals become inconvenient).
- Believing rest was a luxury I couldn't afford (survival becomes negotiable).

Until my body made the decision for me. Cloud and Townsend describe boundaries like a fence around your home: They show what's yours to protect and what isn't.

Research[37] identifies seven types of boundaries: material, internal, conversational, physical, time, mental and emotional. I had work to do in every single one, but I started where the pain was sharpest: time.

My diary was a free-for-all. Eight back-to-back meetings on Monday, seven on Tuesday, all-day workshops on Wednesday. By Friday, I was running on fumes.

But I told myself this was what senior leaders did. We showed up. We said 'yes'. We made ourselves available.

What I didn't realise: I'd confused being available with being valuable.

I never thought to challenge what role I would have in meetings and whether they were a valuable use of my time, nor the physical reality that I couldn't simply retain excellence with eight back-to-back meetings a day!

I didn't feel I could push back and decline a meeting as I feared not being valued, displeasing or not supporting my team.

I decided to take control back of my diary.

I would look at my week ahead critically and decide which meetings were truly important, which ones I needed to decline and which ones I needed to understand my role in them so I could make an informed decision. I also started to block out time to do my thinking work. I held this boundary even when people felt they could pop a meeting in over the top. I would sense-check where I focused my energy, be disciplined about where my time was spent and make sure I had gaps in between a big day of meetings where I could rest, go to the bathroom and even eat lunch!

I also realised I had to come up with clear responses for how I would say no or decline a meeting.

I needed scripts — actual phrases I could practise and deploy without having to think through the guilt every time.

'I'd love to come to that meeting. Can you help me understand my role?'

Translation: Is this meeting necessary, and do you actually need me?

'I'm not available at that time.'

No explanation. No excuse. Just: not available. This one took practise. My people-pleaser self wanted to add 15 reasons why.

'Let me suggest who could attend in my place.'

Making sure the right person was in the room, not just the most senior.

These phrases formed the architecture of a new operating system. Each one protected something essential: my energy, my focus, my capacity to keep showing up.

And here's what shocked me: The more consistently I held them, the more people respected them.

Here is the simple process I went through to get clear on my boundaries:

- *Define what the boundaries are.* What is okay or not okay for me at work and home, and why.
- *Communicate* what my newly reset boundaries were with others.
- *Design some key phrases* to help navigate a boundary being tested.
- *Don't over-explain* them, just own them.
- *Set the consequences* for myself and others when the boundaries were not honoured.

Your boundaries aren't suggestions, they're requirements for sustainable excellence. They're not walls keeping people out. They're the architecture that keeps you functioning at your best.

Every time you negotiate them away, you're training everyone around you — including yourself — that your limits are flexible and your needs are optional.

They're not.

Boundaries protect what matters, but boundaries alone aren't enough.

You also need practices — the daily disciplines that allow you to show up consistently within those boundaries. The rituals that sustain your energy, sharpen your focus and keep you operating at your best without running yourself into the ground.

This is where the theory becomes lived reality. Where sustainable excellence stops being an aspiration and starts being how you actually operate.

Embodying sustainable practices

Here's the difference between practices that stick and the ones you abandon by February: Embodied practices become part of you, not just another thing on your to-do list.

These aren't fads you try because someone said they worked for them. They're not 'shoulds' you force yourself to do. They're practices that light you up because, deep down, you know they work for *you*. The ones that, once you start doing them, become so fundamental to how you show up that you actually miss them when they're gone.

That's when you know a practice is embodied: When it stops being something you have to remember and starts being something you can't imagine living without. When it becomes part of your DNA. When it's not discipline any more, it's just how you operate.

These are the practices that make sustainable success possible. The foundations that allow you to achieve your ambition without it costing you everything. Not because they're revolutionary or complex, but because they're genuinely yours. They work for you, not against you.

This is about finding what actually sustains you, and doing it consistently enough that it becomes who you are, not just what you do.

I learned this the hard way.

When you're receiving daily radiation and still need to keep a roof over your head, you don't have the luxury of pushing through. You have to design a completely different way of working.

So I became a student of sustainable high performance. For six months, I deep dived into productivity methods, energy management research and performance psychology, testing everything to see what actually worked for my body and my life.

I knew I needed cornerstones — non-negotiables that would form the foundation, such as:

- energy management over time management
- being able to identify high-impact activities (the 20 per cent that creates 80 per cent)
- rest as strategy, not reward
- doing the most important things, not everything
- being adaptable and working with my body's ups and downs
- natural rhythms: finding flow
- intentional spaciousness that gave me time to think, be present, enjoy life.

Here's what also became crystal clear: less, done well, with focus and intention, creates more impact than more done frantically while depleted. One brilliant hour of focused work in your peak energy window delivers more value than three exhausted hours of distracted effort.

For a week at a time, I tested practices. At the end of each week, I assessed: Did this work? Keep or let it go?

The 5 am club didn't last: I was too drugged from meds to function well at that hour. The zero-inbox method didn't work: emails are de-energisers for me.

So I became a detective of my own energy.

Discovering my rhythms

I tracked: When did I feel sharp? When did brain fog hit? Which tasks lit me up? Which ones drained me like a vampire? What time of day was my superpower hour?

Patterns emerged:

- *Best brain:* 9 am to 11.30 am (this is when I do strategy work, writing, make big decisions)
- *Energy crashes:* 4 pm (this is when I batch admin tasks or take proper breaks, not fight my body)
- *Second wind:* sometime around 2 pm (but only if I haven't pushed through all day).

Working with these rhythms instead of against them changed everything.

I learned about ultradian rhythms, which showed me that our bodies naturally cycle through 90- to 120-minute periods of high focus followed by 15- to 20-minute recovery periods. Tony Schwartz's work with high performers shows that when we push through our days without respecting our natural rhythms, we gradually drain our physical and mental capacity—a slow erosion of energy that ultimately limits our effectiveness.[38]

I stopped working longer than 90 minutes at a time for focused work. I did my thinking work when my brain was at an optimum (before 11 am). I did sprints of focused work. I batched my emails three times a day. I did less important tasks at lower energy points, usually around 4 pm.

I worked when my body felt strongest and rested when it didn't.

And here's the thing: Surrendering to rest, taking regular breaks throughout the day, meant I could actually do more for longer. Catching fatigue dips and taking ten-minute breaks allowed me to bounce back and keep going.

Reset challenge #7: Know your energy truth

Become an energy detective to discover your own unique patterns and rhythms. For one week, track these four things daily:

1. Peak performance windows

When do you feel sharpest? Most creative? Most able to tackle complex problems? Note the time, what you were doing, what preceded it. You're looking for patterns. Maybe you're brilliant 9 am to 11 am but foggy after lunch. Maybe Sunday mornings are your strategic thinking goldmine.

2. Recovery signals

What does your body/mind do when it needs a break? Notice: restlessness, snacking, scrolling, irritability, staring at the same email for ten minutes, headaches.

3. Energy enablers

What activities, people or environments actually give you energy while you're doing them? Simply notice them and note them down.

4. Energy drainers

What consistently drains you, even when it's 'supposed' to be easy? Be honest. Maybe email drains you. Maybe certain meetings. Maybe that person you're trying to please. This isn't about judgement, it's about radical honesty.

Then ask yourself:

- How could I plan my week around my natural energy rhythms?
- How can I schedule draining tasks when I'm most resilient?
- How can I protect my peak energy for my most important work?
- What boundaries would protect my energy most effectively?

Reading the warning signs

I also needed to understand what triggered me to switch into over-functioning and overdrive. I found anything that had the word 'over' in it typically meant I had fallen into a state of exhaustion rather than from a place of excellence. Whenever I started to over-polish a presentation, or over-function for my team by jumping in and fixing issues, or when I over-pleased by saying 'yes' during a client meeting, I realised that I had fallen into overdrive.

I put in simple practices at the start and end of each day. I spent 15 minutes before I looked at my emails, planning out my most important tasks of the day and setting my intention for the day ahead. And at the end of my day, I took ten to 15 minutes to reflect on the day that was, celebrating what I had achieved and what I needed to focus on tomorrow.

Simple, daily, sustainable practices that allowed me to catch and reset. Making sure I focused on what mattered and didn't get swept up in the busy, defaulting into pushing and proving, ending the week utterly exhausted.

I did the same exercise every month, every quarter and year. I got clear on what excellence looked like for the time period ahead, set my intention, my goals and practices that were going to allow me to achieve what mattered sustainably. And it stuck.

Reset challenge #8: Your reality check

Get brutally honest about where you're actually operating right now across all three elements that will allow you to achieve excellence without exhaustion. Before you design your system, you need to know where you are right now. Grab your journal. Take a moment to honestly reflect on these questions:

Self-fullness check:

- Does my work energise me or drain me by the day's end?
- Am I operating from abundance or borrowing against my future self?
- Do I wake up with energy for what matters, or am I already running on empty?

Boundaries check:

- Are my boundaries holding under pressure or collapsing?
- Am I honouring what works for me, or abandoning it when things get intense?
- Do I feel grounded in who I am, or as though I'm wearing a mask?

Embodied practices check:

- Am I choosing how I respond or just reacting to what's screaming loudest?
- Do I have clarity and perspective, or am I constantly firefighting?
- Am I working with my rhythms or fighting my body all day?

Write down what you notice. What patterns are showing up? What's the gap between where you are and where you want to be?

The way of tea

The most powerful surprising practice for me was the silent tea ceremony at Cloud Hidden, a tea house where 18 people sit in silence for 60 minutes while a tea master serves five rounds of tea with intention.

The name itself captured what I felt I needed. It was like being on an airplane when you rise above the clouds and find blue sky, letting the noisy clouds of life settle so you can see clearly what matters.

It became like a gym membership. I'd sit there three or more times a week to be with my thoughts. To reflect. To quieten the busy overachiever within. To just be. To literally and metaphorically fill my cup.

This simple regular practice changed me. Not because sitting in silence is magical, but because I finally gave myself permission to stop, to settle, to simply be.

What matters is that you find the practice that allows you space to notice how you're really showing up, to retain perspective and clarity on what actually matters.

My system in action

Here's what my operating system actually looks like. Table 10.1 is not a template to copy, but proof that designing your own is possible.

Table 10.1 An example of system in action

When	What I do	Why it works for me
Morning (7–10 am)	Wake at 7 am consistently	Consistent wake time regulates my body's rhythm
	Drink coffee in sun (no phone)	Morning sun activates my body naturally
	Ten minutes of reading	
	Head to the gym at 8 am	I move in the morning, by evening, I'm done
	Plan my day	
	Start work at 10 am	Peak brain energy 9–11.30 am protected
During the day	Email batching (15 minutes at 10 am, 1 pm and 4 pm)	Emails are de-energisers for me
	Ten-minute breaks between meetings	No back-to-back meetings ever
	Focused sprints (45 to 90 minutes at a time)	Work with ultradian rhythms
	Maximum four meetings a day	More than four meetings = ineffective
	One look-forward-to moment daily	Keeps me motivated

When	What I do	Why it works for me
Weekly rhythm	Monday: Warm-up	Matches my natural energy arc
	Tuesday: Power day (most important tasks)	Protects Tuesday peak performance
	Wednesday: Meetings	New business, client meetings
	Thursday: Workshop, coaching or presentation delivery	In-room with leaders or new business
	Friday: Wind down (finish 1 pm)	The lighter day; reflect on the week; space to be and plan the week ahead; wrap up any tasks; finish early
End of day	Review planner (15 minutes)	Consciously bookending the day with intentional reflection creates closure
	Reflect on wins/learnings	
	Plan tomorrow's most important tasks	
	'Come off the mountain' (menial tasks, walk, tea ceremony)	Brain needs to de-activate
	Dim lights 7 pm	
	Wind-down routine	Signals to the body that it's time to rest
	Bedtime 10–10.30 pm	Consistent sleep time is crucial

(continued)

Table 10.1   An example of system in action (*cont'd*)

When	What I do	Why it works for me
Non-negotiables	Ten-minute morning stillness Exercise, breathwork, tea ceremony Bookending each day One look-forward-to moment weekly No meetings before 10 am	These five practices are my foundation. Everything else can flex; these cannot.

What makes this work: It honours my energy patterns (peak 9 am to 11.30 am, crash 4 pm), protects recovery (ten-minute breaks, no back-to-back meetings) and includes what lights me up (look-forward-to moments, tea ceremony).

My system, not a template

Here's what you need to understand: My system is my system.

What works for me won't necessarily work for you because your body, mind and soul are different. Your energy patterns are different. Your boundaries need to protect different things. What fills your cup might be completely different from what fills mine. And that's exactly how it should be.

The 5 am club didn't work for me, but it might be perfect for you. Email batching three times a day is my rhythm, yours might be different. The silent tea ceremony is my grounding practice, yours might be running, painting, journalling or sitting with your dog.

The universal truth that underpins every sustainable system is that less done well beats more done at the cost of you. Always. Every high performer I've worked with resists this at first. We're conditioned to believe more equals better. But volume without focus is just sophisticated busy work. Impact comes from doing fewer things brilliantly, not everything adequately.

The point isn't to copy my system, it's to design yours.

Here's what I know to be universal, what I've seen work for thousands of overachievers desperate for a better way.

Self-fullness isn't optional, it's strategic

You can't give what you don't have. Operating from depletion might feel noble, but it's not sustainable. Fill your cup first, not because you're selfish, but because you're smart.

Boundaries aren't walls, they're the architecture of sustainable excellence

The boundaries you don't hold will eventually be forced upon you, usually by your body, your relationships or a crisis you didn't see coming. Define them now, while you still have the choice.

Embodied practices aren't nice-to-haves, they're your operating system

Design your days with the same rigour you'd apply to a business strategy. Work with your body's rhythms, not against them. Build in recovery. Create systems that make excellence your default, not something you have to fight for every day.

Tips for finding your practices:

- *Start your day with you first:* Figure out what sets you up for a good day. As Tim Ferriss says, 'if you win the morning, you win the day'.
- *Trial and error:* Don't be discouraged if the first practices don't stick. Stay curious. Your gut will tell you what works.
- *Tune into your body rhythms:* Set consistent wake/sleep times first, then track your energy throughout the day.

- *Practise for a week:* Stick to whatever you try for at least seven days before deciding that it doesn't work or you need to change it.
- *Determine your non-negotiables:* Pick one to two game-changing practices you know work and make them actually happen.

Keep freshening up: Commit to new practices for at least 21 days. Then evolve them. Constant iteration keeps them interesting.

Start small with one practice a week to test and learn, then begin to build a series of practices that you believe make a real difference to how you work and lead. Stick with them for 30 days and see what shifts. Then decide what to embody as your new way of operating and release what doesn't.

Perhaps you already have some practices that you do now. Take some time to review them. Sense-check whether they are resulting in excellence without exhaustion or whether there is some room to improve them. Let go of the practices that are no longer serving you and bring in one new practice to trial to freshen things up.

What I know to be true

✧ You don't have to choose between excellence and exhaustion. You don't have to sacrifice your health for your ambition or your joy for your goals. The old playbook that got you this far—the grinding, the yes-to-everything mentality, the belief that rest is for the weak—isn't serving you any more.

✧ There's a different way, and it is about doing less. Less done well is more impactful than more done at the cost of you and what matters.

✧ When you build a system that honours your body, mind, and soul, when you operate from self-fullness, hold brave boundaries and design practices that work with your rhythms, everything becomes possible. Not just sustainable, but actually energising.

✧ You'll finish your days with energy still left to enjoy your life. You'll have capacity for the people and moments that matter. You'll create exceptional results without destroying yourself in the process.

✧ Your decisions get clearer because you're not making them from depletion. Your impact multiplies because you're not constantly recovering from overdrive.

And here's what I didn't expect: once you build this system, you never go back. Not because you're disciplined (as you already are), but because you finally discover what it feels like when your ambition and your sense of self can co-exist, when the right support structure and intentional choices make sustainable excellence possible.

This changed my life in ways I can't even fully articulate. It was the unlock I needed in the hardest of times, and it became the foundation for everything that followed.

Reset challenge #9: Designing your system

Now it's time to build your operating system using the three elements and your energy discovery data. Start with one practice in each element and build from there. After your week of discovery, you have the raw data. Now architect your system.

Element 1: Self-fullness

Pick one thing in each area to trial for a week for your:

- body (movement, rest, nourishment)
- mind (learning, creating, space to think)
- soul (connection, beauty, meaning)

Examples: Going for a walk with a loved one, planning your day, simple stretches, breathwork to calm your nervous system, journalling, playing with your kids/dog

Element 2: Brave boundaries

- What's the one boundary you most need to set or strengthen right now?
- What specific phrase will you use when this boundary is tested?
- How will holding this boundary protect your energy and impact?

Examples: No meetings before 10 am, 'I'm not available at that time', not looking at your phone/emails for the first half hour of the day so your body and brain can wake up fully

Element 3: Embodied practices (Based on your energy discovery)

- What's your peak performance window (when you're sharpest)?
- Which practice will you trial for 30 days to work with your rhythms (not against them)?
- What will you do when you notice your 'over' warning signs (reset protocol)?

Example: Peak 9–11.30 am; Focused sprints + ten-minute breaks; Stop, take a break, reassess

Start with one thing in each area. Trial it for a week, see how it lands, adjust, then build from there. My system took months to develop. Yours will take time too. That's the process. Excellence without exhaustion is a practice, not a destination.

Once you've built your system across all three elements, you'll have the architecture that sustains your brilliance, not by forcing yourself to be disciplined, but by designing a way of working that makes sustainable excellence your default.

✨ Glittering truths ✨

If you only remember three things from this chapter, make them these:

1. Self-fullness is strategic, not selfish

You can't give what you don't have. Every time you put yourself last, you're teaching everyone around you (including yourself) that your needs are optional. They're not. Fill your own cup first. Not because you're self-indulgent, but because you're smart. When you operate from abundance rather than depletion, you have more to give, and it costs you less to give it. Self-fullness isn't optional, it's the foundation everything else is built on.

2. Boundaries are the protectors of sustainable excellence

They're not walls, they're the framework that protects your capacity to keep showing up at your best. The boundaries you don't hold will eventually be forced upon you, usually by your body, your relationships or a crisis you didn't see coming. Define them now, while you still have the choice. What's okay? What's not okay? Your boundaries aren't suggestions, they're requirements for sustainable excellence.

3. Excellence requires architecture, not willpower

Embodied practices aren't nice-to-haves, they're your operating system. You can't white-knuckle your way to sustainable high performance. You need daily practices that work with your body, not against it. Design your days with the same rigour you'd apply to a business strategy. Build in recovery. Work with your rhythms. Create systems that make excellence your default, not something you have to fight for every single day.

CONCLUSION: STILL IN THE WAITING ROOM LIVING FULLY

'Live life as if everything is rigged in your favour.'

—*Rumi*

As I write this, I have another scan coming up next week as I'm experiencing another flare. Gong through the familiar dance with medical appointments, blood tests and that peculiar cocktail of hope and dread that comes with chronic illness. The truth is, I'll probably always be in some version of a waiting room — waiting for results, waiting for things to change, waiting to see if this body of mine decides to cooperate or remind me who is boss again.

But here's what's changed everything: I've stopped waiting for certainty to start living fully. I've let go of trying to control the impossible and I choose how I show up for life no matter what happens. I'm enjoying the ride more and proving myself less. I'm tuning into my conscious joy, following my heart, letting go of what doesn't matter and simply living well.

I used to think that once I got better, once I achieved the next milestone, once I had it all sorted, then I'd really begin. Then I'd enjoy the success I'd worked so hard for. Then I'd be present with my family. Then I'd travel, laugh, dance, wear the good dress, use the expensive candles.

Life had other plans … and thank goodness it did.

I have done the work, and it's been far from easy. It's been an intentional way of showing up no matter what life throws at me. Sitting in my grief and accepting my reality. Owning my ambition and desires to make my one precious life matter. And never forgetting to enjoy the simple pleasures every day I can get out of bed to enjoy it.

I'm still in the waiting room of uncertainty, but I'm no longer waiting for my life to begin. I'm living it — all of it — right now. I had no idea that this wellbeing journey, redefining my life (not at the cost of me) would be the greatest gift of my life.

The real victory

This book isn't about beating illness or achieving perfect work-life balance or becoming the leader who never struggles. That's not the victory I'm celebrating. The real victory is much quieter and infinitely more radical:

Not perfect health, but authentic living. I may never get the guarantee of a perfectly healthy future, but I've learned to live fully in an imperfect present. I've stopped waiting for my body to be 'normal' to live fully.

Not arrival, but presence. I used to think success meant reaching a destination where I'd finally feel 'enough'. Now I know that enough isn't a place you arrive at, it's a choice you make every single day with intention, to be present to what is, rather than always chasing what's next.

Not performance, but deep inner peace. The greatest shift wasn't learning to achieve without exhaustion (though that did change everything), it was learning that my worth isn't tied to my output.

That I can be valuable without even achieving. That I can rest without earning it.

Fleeting moments, deep contentment. True, deep, heartfelt contentment comes from self-love and compassion. Owning all that you are and being okay with it, celebrating what makes you you. Showing up without efforting to be someone else — that's where real contentment lies. I am happier than I have ever been, and it's stuck.

These weren't the victories I was chasing when I started this journey. These are better. These are lasting, meaningful parts of my precious life that I am so proud to have found. It took me losing my health, having to sit on my ass, and leaning into my greatest teacher — this illness — to discover what life meant for me.

You are the evidence

You are reading this, which means you're ready. Ready to stop performing success and start experiencing it. Ready to lead authentically rather than perfectly. Ready to build something meaningful without destroying yourself in the process.

Don't delay, my love. Life is for living. Now is now.

Here's what I need you to understand: *My life is proof that a different way exists despite what happens to you.* It's not a perfect way, it's not an easy way, but it's a sustainable way. A way that includes you in the equation of your own success.

I am not extraordinary. I'm not superhuman. I don't have special powers or secret knowledge. I'm an overachiever who broke, just like you might be breaking. The only difference is that I chose to do the real work to find a better way — a way that was not at the cost of me. I refused to give up and did the inner work on my mindset, and then shaped my life to follow suit, consistently every day.

And if I can learn to do it differently, if I can learn to create greater impact by doing less, honour my body's limits, marry my mind and body to work as one, show up fully as myself, choose conscious joy daily and give back the lessons that cost me so much to learn... then you can choose your own version of sustainable success before life forces the choice on you.

You don't have to wait for a crisis to give you permission to live differently

Your reset will become evidence for someone else. The person watching you lead with authenticity instead of anxiety. The colleague who sees you setting boundaries without guilt. The loved one who witnesses you enjoying your achievements instead of immediately chasing the next ones.

You'll never know whose life you change by choosing to do success differently. But you will change lives. Starting with your own.

When you stop being a martyr for your ambition, you give everyone around you permission to do the same. When you lead from your high impact state instead of your high cost state, your team learns what sustainable excellence actually looks like. When you choose conscious joy as part of your leadership, you create cultures where people bring their whole selves to work.

This isn't just about you any more, it's about the legacy you're creating through how you choose to succeed

I think about my daughter, watching me work from the kitchen table during treatment, seeing me choose to show up authentically rather than perfectly. I think about my team, learning that vulnerability isn't weakness and that asking for help isn't failure. I think about the leaders I coach, discovering that they can achieve their biggest goals without sacrificing their health, relationships or who they are.

Walking your talk, not just giving advice

The world needs your authentic success. The real you. Not the Instagram version where everything looks effortless and perfectly curated. It needs the real version where you're brilliant and struggling, achieving and learning, succeeding and still becoming.

Your authentic success gives others permission to stop performing their way through life and start living it.

I'm still the woman who gets her whole workshop dancing because living fully and choosing joy is revolutionary in a world that takes itself too seriously.

I'm still the leader who wears sequins to business meetings because life is too short to save the good stuff for special occasions.

I'm still the overachiever who believes in chasing big ambition despite it all and creating meaningful impact in this one precious life I have.

'Doing me' no matter what is so much less exhausting than trying to be this other illusion of perfection.

I'm just doing it all from a place of sustainable excellence instead of self-sacrifice. From high impact instead of high cost. From authenticity instead of performance.

And I'm still in waiting rooms, still facing uncertainty, still navigating the complexities of ambition while living with chronic illness.

But I'm no longer waiting for my life to begin.

I'm living it — all of it — fully, right now.

And so can you.

The reset starts when you decide it starts. The different way becomes possible the moment you choose it. The beautiful beginning happens right now, exactly as you are, wherever you are.

You are the evidence that a different way is possible.

Now go and prove it.

This is your life. This is your reset. This is your beautiful beginning.

Fleur

The Overachiever's Mantra

This is who I am.

*I am enough already... No more proving, no more chasing,
no more performing..*

*I am perfectly imperfect, a magnificent work in becoming
who I was meant to be.*

I operate within my limits and choose sequins over superwoman.

I choose conscious joy over relentless doing.

I tune into what I need and know, deep down, I truly deserve it.

I am brave enough to withstand any storm.

Worthy of love that doesn't need earning.

*I practise radical acceptance and self-compassion,
especially when life gets messy.*

*I celebrate the little moments that actually make a life... the gold
found in ordinary days.*

I have a resilient spirit forged in waiting rooms and boardrooms.

I am stronger than I think. I can handle anything life throws at me.

I trust that life is rigged in my favour, especially when it tests me.

*For I know that in the darkness and messy parts of life is
where I grow and find real meaning.*

*I focus on what matters and own what I can control, letting go
of what I can't.*

I choose less over more, impact over effort, presence over performance.

I own all that I am ... the magnificent and sparkly me.

*I live fully every day I can put my feet on the ground, knowing
this moment is enough already.*

*I have permanently traded in my cape for glitter as I discovered
that I was always enough as I am.*

May you find your own sequins. May you discover that operating within your
limits isn't limiting — it's liberating and life-changing. And may you finally feel
free to sparkle exactly as you are, knowing that you are and always will be
more than enough.

THE JOURNEY DOESN'T END HERE

If you've enjoyed *The Overachiever's Reset* and want to dive deeper into this journey, I invite you to explore more ways to work with me and continue your reset. Head to fleurmarks.com.au for a reset toolbox of resources to help you stay on the path. There's daily check-in practices, reset tools and more. Whether you're looking for open programs you can attend as an individual, tailored corporate leadership programs or personalised coaching, you'll find it all there.

For live events and keynote speaking engagements, there's also a Speaker Playbook. Let's connect on socials too at @fleurjmarks! Follow me to receive reset nudges, musings and tips to show up fully as a leader in your life. And be sure to tag me when sharing your biggest insights from *The Overachiever's Reset* — I'd love to hear what has landed for you.

Life will challenge us at different points — it's what makes us human. When it does, please know you can reach out to me. I mean it. Email me at fleur@fleurmarks.com.au or dive into the reset toolbox — the micro reset practices can help you navigate whatever life throws at you. You don't have to do this alone.

I'm genuinely grateful you picked up this book. My hope is that it has shifted something within you, and that you now see there is a better way to succeed without losing yourself in the process. You deserve to achieve your ambitions and enjoy your life. Both. Not one or the other.

fleurmarks.com.au

Instagram: @fleurjmarks

Facebook: FleurMarks

LinkedIn: linkedin.com/in/fleurmarks/

Email: fleur@fleurmarks.com.au

FURTHER RESOURCES

To get immediate support with mental wellbeing:

- Lifeline (ph 13 11 14, lifeline.org.au): Anyone across Australia experiencing a personal crisis or thinking about suicide can call Lifeline.
- Sane (sane.org): A national Australian mental health organisation for people with complex mental health issues, and for the families and friends who support them.
- Suicide Call Back Service (ph 1300 659 467, suicidecallbackservice.org.au): A free nationwide service providing 24/7 phone and online counselling to people affected by suicide.
- Beyond Blue (ph 1300 22 4636, beyondblue.org.au): Mental health support services for anxiety, depression and suicide.
- Relationships Australia (ph 1300 364 277, relationships.org .au): Relationship support services for individuals, families and communities.
- Healthdirect (healthdirect.gov.au/mental-health-where-to-get-help): Government website where and how to get help and advice about mental health.

To get support for sarcoidosis:

- Foundation for Sarcoidosis Research (stopsarcoidosis.org/fsr-sarcoidosis-support-group/): Online, peer-led support group.
- National Organisation for Rare Disorders (rarediseases.org): For support and information on rare diseases.
- Sarcoidosis and Lyme Disease Support Group Australia (sarcoidosisaustralia.com): A voluntary organisation established for people, families and caregivers affected by sarcoidosis and Lyme disease.
- Life and Breath Foundation for Sarcoidosis (lifeandbreath .org): Dedicated to educating and assisting sarcoidosis patients and their caregivers.

To get support for breast cancer:

- Breast Cancer Support Network (bcna.org.au): Works to ensure all Australians affected by breast cancer receive the very best care, treatment and support.
- Surviving Breast Cancer (survivingbreastcancer.org): Another resource to help you navigate breast cancer and thrive.

ACKNOWLEDGEMENTS

Pete, my hubby, thank you for the endless cups of tea, reading chapters that must have been confronting to relive, and reassuring me when I wobbled about my enoughness to write this book. I love you.

To my two children, Isabella and Luca: Thank you for giving me permission to share our story, including the messy bits about being a sick mum who wanted to be perfect. You taught me that being me was enough. Your *kia kaha* to navigate life's challenges so young has made you such incredible humans. Watching you grow up and find your way in the world, I am in awe as you are so brave, loving and amazing. Please always remember I love you and you, too, are enough exactly as you are.

To my family: Mum, your strength and belief taught me I can do anything, even write a book! You've inspired me, held me and shown me what it means to keep going when life nearly broke me. John, my stepdad, your unconditional love truly shaped me to be who I am and how to be a great hugger! I'm so deeply grateful for your presence in my life. Dad, you taught me to show up and work hard for what I want — you've shaped me more than you know. Tania, my darling sister, thank you for cheering me on every week we talked while also worrying about how hard I worked. Thank you for always being in my corner since we were little and reminding me of what matters. Kimmy, I felt you looking down on me beaming with pride and cheering me on as I wrote this book. I wish you were here every single day.

I acknowledge my whakapapa to Ngāti Kauwhata and Ngāti Kuia — a heritage that influenced me throughout my upbringing, though from a distance, and whose resilience I felt resonate within me when facing adversity, even without speaking fluent te reo Māori. This book honours my Māori culture as something I have always felt within me, and marks a continuing journey of understanding I now share with my children as we learn together what it means to be uri of these iwi.

Professor Carr: Without you in my corner, I would not be here. Fifteen years is a hell of a ride. Thank you for being brilliant at what you do and always responding to my emails despite thousands of patients needing you. To all my 'ologists' and the nurses at St Vincent's Hospital who administered chemo, countless infusions and surgeries — thank you for making me welcome no matter what shape I showed up in, and for letting me wear sequins to treatment!

Natasha, my therapist: Without your support over the last 15 years, this book simply wouldn't exist. You've seen me at my worst and helped me learn a better way. You are the reason I do what I do now — the wisdom and tools in this book are the ones you taught me first. You've always reminded me of my enoughness; caught me when I fell back into old learned patterns; and taught me how to redefine, reset and rediscover my life. You are my wise mind always, and I am so lucky to have you.

Donna and Rachel: Two of my besties and beta readers who've walked this 15-year journey with me. Fellow overachievers with busy jobs who still showed up in the darkest moments, watched trashy TV, held my hand and loved me as I am. And to Mitch, Hendo, Janine, Tessa, Jana, Mira, Katie, Linda and so many other incredible women who reminded me of what mattered. You know who you are.

Janine Garner: You held my hand on every step of this book journey and wouldn't let go. You encouraged me to put my story on paper when I doubted anyone would care, kept me on the path when I wanted to give up, and talked me through every moment my health tested my resolve. Your belief in me, my story and getting this out there is why this book actually exists. Thank you for reading the manuscript and giving honest feedback to make it better, and for connecting me with the incredible support I needed to make this happen. You made this real.

Kelly Irving: You're an incredible book coach who helped me find structure in the fog. Thank you for the honest feedback about writing not one but four books, for helping me strike the right balance between my story and the reader's journey, and for the cake analogy that finally made it click. You helped me get this book to a place I'm proud of.

To the Wiley family: Lucy Raymond for believing in this book, Leigh for your patience, Melanie for your wisdom and kindness as my copy editor, Chris for keeping this book on path, Renee for your marketing expertise, and the entire Wiley crew for making this happen.

Scott Eathorne: Thank you for getting this into as many hands as possible as a media genius.

To my case study contributors for their vulnerability; the Elevate women and all the amazing women and leaders who have cheered me on to keep showing up over the last 15 years; my clients who let me test my methodology on their leaders; and my online community for following my journey, sharing vulnerably and encouraging me.

Poppy and Lola: My fur babies who remind me what unconditional love looks like and that every day is about nature and balls.

And to *you*, my overachiever. You are the reason I do what I do. Thank you for picking up this book and entrusting me to guide you. My wish is that it wakes you up to the possibility of achieving without losing yourself, so you can actually enjoy this crazy wild ride called life.

Always remember: you are enough already.

REFERENCES

1. Priestley, A 2025, 'A 2025 reality: Majority of women report burnout', Women's Agenda, Retrieved from https://womensagenda.com.au/latest/eds-blog/a-2025-reality-majority-of-women-report-burnout/.
2. Tilo D 2024, 'Burnout epidemic: New report reveals 80 per cent of Australians feel burnt out', HRD Australia, Retrieved from https://www.hcamag.com/au/specialisation/leadership/burnout-epidemic-new-report-reveals-80-of-australians-feel-burnt-out/515587.
3. Magennis M 2024, 'More than 30 per cent of Australians likely to quit their job in the next year, Allianz Australia research finds', 7News, Retrieved from https://7news.com.au/news/more-than-30-per-cent-of-australians-likely-to-quit-their-job-in-the-next-year-allianz-australia-research-finds--c-15015957.
4. Clance, PR and Imes, SA 1978, 'The imposter phenomenon in high achieving women: Dynamics and therapeutic intervention', *Psychotherapy: Theory, Research and Practice*, vol. 15, no. 3, pp. 241–7.
5. Brown, B 2010, *The gifts of imperfection: Let go of who you think you're supposed to be and embrace who you are*, Hazelden Publishing.
6. Young, JE, Klosko, JS and Weishaar, ME 2003, *Schema therapy: A practitioner's guide*, Guilford Press.
7. Jung, CG 1966, *Two essays on analytical psychology, trans.* R.F.C. Hull, Princeton University Press.
8. Maslach, C and Jackson, SE 1981, 'The measurement of experienced burnout', *Journal of Organizational Behavior*, vol. 2, no. 2, pp. 99–113.
9. Ibarra, YH 1999, 'Provisional selves: Experimenting with image and identity in professional adaptation', *Administrative Science Quarterly*, vol. 44, no. 4, pp. 764–91.
10. Sapir, E 1929, 'The status of linguistics as a science', *Language*, vol. 5, no. 4, pp. 207–14.

11. Baumeister, RF and Vohs, KD 2007, 'Self-regulation, ego depletion, and motivation', *Social and Personality Psychology Compass*, vol. 1, no. 1, pp. 115–28.

12. Cloud, H and Townsend, J 2017, *Boundaries: When to say yes, how to say no to take control of your life*, HarperChristian Resources.

13. Arnsten, AFT 2009, 'Stress signalling pathways that impair prefrontal cortex structure and function', *Nature Reviews Neuroscience*, vol. 10, no. 6, pp. 410–22.

14. McEwen, BS 1998, 'Stress, adaptation, and disease: Allostasis and allostatic load', *Annals of the New York Academy of Sciences*, vol. 840, no. 1, pp. 33–44.

15. Wood, W and Rünger, D 2016, 'Psychology of habit', *Annual Review of Psychology*, vol. 67, pp. 289–314.

16. Carver, CS, Scheier, MF and Weintraub, JK 1989, 'Assessing coping strategies: A theoretically based approach', *Journal of Personality and Social Psychology*, vol. 56, no. 2, pp. 267–83.

17. Schultz, W 2016, 'Dopamine reward prediction error coding', *Dialogues in Clinical Neuroscience*, vol. 18, no. 1, pp. 23–32.

18. Selye, S 1946, 'The general adaptation syndrome and the diseases of adaptation', *Journal of Clinical Endocrinology*, vol. 6, no. 2, pp. 117–230.

19. Flett, GL, Hewitt, PL and Dyck, T 2016, 'Perfectionism, psychopathology, and vulnerability to stress', in *Perfectionism, Health, and Well-Being*, ed. Fuschia M. Sirois and Danielle S. Molnar, Springer.

20. Lupien, SJ, Maheu, F, Tu, M, Fiocco, A and Schramek, TE 2007, 'The effects of stress and stress hormones on human cognition: Implications for the field of brain and cognition', *Brain and Cognition*, vol. 65, no. 3, pp. 209–37.

21. Maslach, C and Jackson, SE 1981, 'The measurement of experienced burnout', *Journal of Organizational Behavior*, vol. 2, no. 2, pp. 99–113.

22. McEwen, BS 1998, 'Protective and damaging effects of stress mediators', *New England Journal of Medicine*, vol. 338, no. 3, pp. 171–9.

23. De Cremer, D 2002, 'Respect and cooperation in social dilemmas: The importance of feeling included', *Personality and Social Psychology Bulletin*, vol. 28, no. 10, pp. 1335–41.

24. Edmondson, AC 1999, 'Psychological safety and learning behavior in work teams', *Administrative Science Quarterly*, vol. 44, no. 2, pp. 350–83.

25. Pontari, BA and Schlenker, BR 2000, 'The influence of cognitive load on self-presentation: Can cognitive busyness help as well as harm social performance?', *Journal of Personality and Social Psychology*, vol. 78, no. 6, pp. 1092–108.

26. Wood, AM, Linley, PA, Maltby, J, Baliousis, M and Joseph, S 2008, 'The authentic personality: A theoretical and empirical conceptualization and the development of the authenticity scale', *Journal of Counseling Psychology,* vol. 55, no. 3, pp. 385–99.

27. Zak, PJ 2017, 'The neuroscience of trust', *Harvard Business Review,* vol. 95, no. 1, pp. 84–90.

28. Wood, AM, Linley, PA, Maltby, J, Baliousis, M and Joseph, S 2008, 'The authentic personality: A theoretical and empirical conceptualization and the development of the authenticity scale', *Journal of Counseling Psychology,* vol. 55, no. 3, pp. 385–99.

29. Edmondson, AC 1999, 'Psychological safety and learning behavior in work teams', *Administrative Science Quarterly,* vol. 44, no. 2, pp. 350–83.

30. Rozovsky, J 2015, 'The five keys to a successful Google team,' Work with Google, Retrieved from https://www.michigan.gov/-/media/Project/ Websites/mdhhs/Folder4/Folder10/Folder3/Folder110/Folder2/ Folder210/Folder1/Folder310/Google-and-Psychological-Safety.pdf? rev=7786b2b9ade041e78828f839eccc8b75.

31. Brach, T n.d., RAIN: Recognize, allow, investigate, nurture, Tara Brach, Retrieved from https://www.tarabrach.com/rain/.

32. Shafran, R, Cooper, Z and Fairburn, CG 2002, 'Clinical perfectionism: A cognitive-behavioural analysis', *Behaviour Research and Therapy,* vol. 40, no. 7, pp. 773–91.

33. Neff, KD 2003, 'Self-Compassion: An alternative conceptualization of a healthy attitude toward oneself', *Self and Identity,* vol. 2, no. 2, pp. 85–101.

34. Harvard Business School Online. (2019, December 10). *Authentic Leadership: Why It's Important and How to Be an Authentic Leader. Business Insights Blog.* Retrieved from https://online.hbs.edu/blog/ post/authentic-leadership.

35. Zak, PJ 2017, 'The neuroscience of trust', *Harvard Business Review,* Retrieved from https://hbr.org/2017/01/the-neuroscience-of-trust.

36. Cloud, H and Townsend, J 1992, *Boundaries: When to say yes, how to say no to take control of your life,* Zondervan.

37. Nash, J 2018, 'How to set healthy boundaries and build positive relationships', Positive Psychology, Retrieved from https:// positivepsychology.com/great-self-care-setting-healthy-boundaries/

38. Loehr, J and Schwartz, T 2003, *The power of full engagement: Managing energy, not time, is the key to high performance and personal renewal,* Free Press.